ROOSEVELT, WILSON, AND THE TRUSTS

Problems in American Civilization

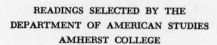

READINGS SELECTED BY THE
DEPARTMENT OF AMERICAN STUDIES
AMHERST COLLEGE

Puritanism in Early America
The Causes of the American Revolution
The Declaration of Independence and the Constitution
Hamilton and the National Debt
The Turner Thesis concerning the Role of the Frontier in American History
Jackson versus Biddle — The Struggle over the Second Bank of the United States
The Transcendentalist Revolt against Materialism
Slavery as a Cause of the Civil War
Democracy and the Gospel of Wealth
John D. Rockefeller — Robber Baron or Industrial Statesman?
Roosevelt, Wilson, and the Trusts
Pragmatism and American Culture
The New Deal — Revolution or Evolution?
Industry-wide Collective Bargaining — Promise or Menace?

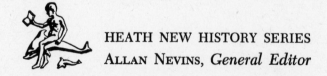

HEATH NEW HISTORY SERIES
ALLAN NEVINS, *General Editor*

Roosevelt, Wilson
and the Trusts

EDITED WITH AN INTRODUCTION BY
Edwin C. Rozwenc

Problems in American Civilization

READINGS SELECTED BY THE
DEPARTMENT OF AMERICAN STUDIES
AMHERST COLLEGE

D. C. HEATH AND COMPANY: Boston

Offices

Boston	New York	Chicago	Dallas
	Atlanta	San Francisco	London

INTRODUCTION

IN 1900 and 1901, American newspapers and periodicals were full of articles celebrating the ending of one century and the beginning of another. While most of these were self-congratulatory reviews of the material achievements of the United States in the previous century — in population, area, industry, invention, and finance — there was also general agreement that advances in art, literature, learning, and law had been equally notable. In the words of one American clergyman, the nineteenth century was a fascinating chapter in the story of "man's upward progress."

However inadequately these effusions depicted the actual conditions of American society, they did, nevertheless, reaffirm an image of American life in the nineteenth century. Millions of European immigrants had come to America attracted by a vision of material prosperity and individual freedom. Generations of native Americans had lived and worked in the hope that something better would happen to Americans than had happened to men in any other country. As Herbert Croly wrote in 1909, "An America which was not the land of promise, which was not informed by a prophetic outlook and a more or less constructive ideal, would not be the America bequeathed to us by our forefathers."[1]

The material achievements which were so clearly evident as America entered the

[1] Herbert D. Croly, *The Promise of American Life* (New York, 1909), p. 3.

twentieth century seemed to confirm the American's vision of a better future. Yet the growth of their cities and the upbuilding of their industrial centers, in which Americans took so much pride, was accompanied by a startling increase, not only in the aggregate wealth of the country, but in the number of large personal fortunes and, particularly, of very large corporate fortunes. This concentration of economic power, more than any other condition in American economic development, contributed to the feeling of anxiety which lay beneath the surface optimism of the speechmaking and editorializing which marked the turn of the century. President Theodore Roosevelt, after paying abundant tribute to American business genius in his first message to Congress, acknowledged that "there is a widespread conviction in the minds of the American people that the great corporations known as trusts are in certain of their features and tendencies hurtful to the general welfare."

As a matter of fact, the great burst of self-congratulatory literature which ushered in the twentieth century was quickly followed by an even more impressive outpouring of critical literature which probed the darker phases of American civilization. So prolific was this literature of protest that the first decade of the twentieth century has been labelled "the era of the muckrakers." Such popular magazines as *McClure's*, *Everybody's*, *Pearson's*, *Cosmopolitan*, and *Collier's* published articles exposing the evils of American society — political corruption, stock market manipulation, fake advertising, vice, impure food and drugs, and race discrimination, to name only a few. This was the era which brought into prominence such journalists as Ida Tarbell, Ray Stannard Baker, Lincoln Steffens, and Charles Edward Russell. These journalists had their counterpart in the field of imaginative literature where writers like Frank Norris, Upton Sinclair, and Jack London depicted the tragedy and brutality of industrial civilization.

To be sure, this kind of criticism was not new. It had already made an appearance in the closing decades of the nineteenth century in such famous works as Henry George's *Progress and Poverty,* Edward Bellamy's *Looking Backward,* and Henry Demarest Lloyd's *Wealth Against Commonwealth.* Yet all three of these social critics were associated with heterodox political movements which cut them off from the majority of the American people. Not only did their ideas seem to be radically new, but the economic strains and the class antagonisms generated by the hard times of the eighties and nineties made them seem dangerous to the established institutions of American society. Hence, the first reaction to this protest by the greater proportion of the American people, particularly the middle classes, was a protective one designed to defend customary institutions and practices from the unknown perils of sweeping change.

On the other hand, the era of the muckrakers was a period of relative prosperity with diminished class antagonisms. After the storms and stresses of the nineties, the opening decade of the twentieth century was a period of fair sailing which permitted some sober second thoughts about the economic and social conditions of the country. It was in such an atmosphere that respectable middle-class men and women gave leadership to reform movements in their states and cities through social service, and by seeking to legislate against political corruption and economic abuses. This was a decade in which Hazen Pingree, Samuel (Golden Rule) Jones, Robert M. La Follette, Woodrow Wilson, Charles Evans Hughes, Jane Addams, and Judge Ben Lindsey, in one way or another joined the quest for a greater measure of social justice. Moreover, the work of reform received added impetus because of the support which it had from Theodore Roosevelt, the leader of the party of respectability and conservatism.

Practically all of the reforming efforts of the period, whether in politics, in law, or in social work, ultimately brought to the reformers a realization of the existence of concentrated economic power in America. The resistance of corporate interests even to moderate reforms provoked Theodore Roosevelt to complain to William Howard Taft in 1906, "The dull, purblind folly of the very rich men; their greed and arrogance . . . and the corruption in business and politics, have tended to produce a very unhealthy condition of excitement and irritation in the popular mind, which shows itself in the great increase in the socialistic propaganda."[2] For this reason, Theodore Roosevelt gave his support to the battle for more effective regulation of the railroads, a pure food and drug law, and the conservation of natural resources. Also, he embarked upon a career of "trustbusting" which seemed to be all the more spectacular coming after a decade of ineffective enforcement of the Sherman Anti-Trust law. Although Theodore Roosevelt

[2] Quoted in Henry F. Pringle, *Theodore Roosevelt* (New York, 1931), p. 413.

did not really believe that "trustbusting" was an adequate solution of the economic problems of the twentieth century and used the big stick against the trusts somewhat sparingly, his vehement rhetoric against the "malefactors of wealth" contributed to the growing popular awareness of the dangers of uncontrolled corporate power. In this way, countless small business enterprisers, as well as discontented western farmers and exploited urban laborers, came to feel that the development of trusts was endangering one of the fundamental purposes of the American experiment which was, as Lincoln had phrased it, "to afford all an unfettered start, and a fair chance in the race of life."

The remarkable progressive upsurge in this decade shook up both of the two major parties and set the stage for the exciting presidential election in 1912. This presidential campaign was spectacular enough because of the appearance of a new party and the three-cornered contest which resulted between William Howard Taft, Theodore Roosevelt, and Woodrow Wilson. Yet, for students of the trust problem, the campaign of 1912 is fascinating also because it presented to the American people an interesting choice of public policies concerning the trusts. In this debate, Theodore Roosevelt emerged as the advocate of a policy of regulating big corporations in the public interest by means of a governmental commission. Roosevelt based his argument on the assumption that the effort to restore competition as it was in the nineteenth century through a law like the Sherman Act was both futile and foolish. Woodrow Wilson, on the other hand, came forward as the champion of a policy to strengthen anti-trust legislation in order to maintain and restore as much competition as possible in every branch of private industry. Wilson himself summed up his position to an Indiana audience in 1912 by saying, "I stand, as the party behind me stands, for regulated competition of a sort that will put the weak upon an equality with the strong."

This brings us to the question raised in this volume. If concentrated corporate power is a standing danger to democracy, which is the better policy to pursue in the light of modern technology and economic methods? Should the government try to create a regulatory commission powerful enough to control big corporations, or should the government try to prevent monopoly by creating a body of laws for the economy "which will look after the men who are on the make rather than the men who are already made?" To put it more briefly, would "regulated monopoly" be preferable to "regulated competition" in the American democracy of the twentieth century?

The selections in this volume have been chosen to help the reader form a judgment on the questions raised in the political debate of 1912. The chapter from Harold U. Faulkner's *American Economic History* sets the stage for this problem with an excellent short summary of the consolidation of American business from the Civil War to World War I as well as a useful review of anti-trust legislation before and after 1912. The chapter from Eliot Jones, *The Trust Problem in the United States,* is also very useful for the approach to this problem because it offers a case study of a "trust"—the United States Steel Corporation. This is very important for the examination of the issues raised in the campaign of 1912 for two reasons: (1) it offers the reader a close look at the complicated structure of a large industrial corporation; (2) the

United States Steel Corporation, as the other readings will show, was used constantly as a stock example in the discussions of the trust problem, 1910–1912.

Theodore Roosevelt's famous *Outlook* article gives the reader one of the fullest and clearest statements of the position he maintained in the campaign of 1912. Similarly, the selections from the "New Freedom" speeches will give the reader a chance to determine how effectively Woodrow Wilson developed his argument.

The testimony of the three business leaders, Judge Elbert Gary, Andrew Carnegie, and George Perkins, is of great interest. Undoubtedly many present-day readers will be astonished to find Andrew Carnegie and other captains of industry calling upon the government to regulate business even to the point of *fixing prices!* This raises a very interesting historical problem. Why were these great industrial leaders so anxious to support a plan for a public commission to regulate industry and so unalterably opposed to more vigorous anti-trust legislation? Did these men hope, as Wilson charged, that they would be able to control the public commission and use it to their advantage? Or was this merely a vague yearning for a corporative state in which monopolistic advantage and a steady return on watered stock could be preserved through the elimination of "wasteful" price competition? Or were they honestly convinced that modern economic and technological conditions would make such a new relationship between government and business beneficial to the whole economy? It is interesting to note, too, how some of the testimony of these businessmen presages the NRA in the first phase of Franklin D. Roosevelt's New Deal.

The testimony of Louis D. Brandeis, the lawyer-reformer, raises interesting questions about the position of Wilson's supporters. Did they have any clear concept of what the restoration of competition meant? Is Brandeis (or Wilson, for that matter) merely talking about a dream world in which myriads of small enterprisers "whet their wits" in fair competition? Does Brandeis, in his answers to questions about the optimum size of corporations, indicate that he has given careful thought to the measures of law and administration that his economic policy would necessitate? Walter Lippmann asks some of these questions in the selection taken from his *Drift and Mastery.*

The selections from George Mowry's *Theodore Roosevelt and the Progressive Movement* and Alpheus Mason's *Brandeis, A Free Man's Life,* are designed to provide some necessary details concerning political activities in 1911 and 1912. Although these two authors have made judgments about some of the questions in this problem, the reader will surely wish to draw his own conclusions on the basis of materials presented in this volume.

Of course, there are some who may be tempted to say, as did William Allen White after the creation of the Federal Trade Commission in the Wilson administration, that the difference between Theodore Roosevelt's "New Nationalism," and Woodrow Wilson's "New Freedom" is the difference between Tweedledum and Tweedledee. Such a conclusion should not be drawn, however, without a satisfactory reckoning with those clauses of the Clayton Anti-Trust Act limiting the ownership of stock in one corporation by another, and forbidding interlocking directorates for certain classes of banking and business corporations. In any case, the debate on the trust issue in 1912 helped to direct the thinking of some Americans to the problem of how to deal with corporate power in a democratic society. Since our own generation is still struggling to find a satisfactory answer to the same question, a careful review of this earlier controversy may help to direct the choices that we must make at mid-century.

CONTENTS

The Clash of Issues

"... The effort to restore competition as it was sixty years ago, and to trust for justice solely to this proposed restoration of competition, is just as foolish as if we should go back to the flintlocks of Washington's continentals as a substitute for modern weapons of precision. . . Our purpose should be, not to strangle business as an incident of strangling combinations, but to regulate big corporations in a thoroughgoing and effective fashion, so as to help legitimate business as an incident to thoroughly and completely safeguarding the interests of the people as a whole."

— Theodore Roosevelt

"I take my stand absolutely, where every progressive ought to take his stand, on the proposition that private monopoly is indefensible and intolerable. And there I will fight my battle. And I know how to fight it. Everybody who has even read the newspapers knows the means by which these men built up their power and created these monopolies. Any decently equipped lawyer can suggest to you statutes by which the whole business can be stopped."

— Woodrow Wilson

"Attempt to sweep the country back into the old era of ruthless competition, which would be the direct consequence of a vigorous enforcement of the Sherman law, and there will return the evils of deceit and fraud in business, violent fluctuations in prices, the deliberate driving to the wall of weak concerns, and the eventual creation of monopolies by survivors."

— George W. Perkins

"... The Democratic party insists that competition can be and should be maintained in every branch of private industry; that competition can be and should be restored in those branches of industry in which it has been suppressed by the trusts; and that, if at any future time monopoly should appear to be desirable in any branch of industry, the monopoly should be a public one —a monopoly owned by the people and not by the capitalists."

— Louis D. Brandeis

Harold Underwood Faulkner:

CONSOLIDATION OF BUSINESS

The Culmination of Laissez Faire

THE half century following the Civil War saw both the culmination of the economic philosophy of *laissez faire* and the reaction against it. All the processes of the American Industrial Revolution were immensely speeded up by the war; but in the rapidly growing industrial and agricultural life unbridled freedom and competition reigned supreme. The *laissez faire* doctrine of Adam Smith and his successors had been accepted as final by the great majority of Americans in the years immediately following the war, and a fitting capstone had been put upon the theories by the first section of the fourteenth amendment.[1] Although this had supposedly been incorporated in the Constitution to protect the Negro, the increasing pressure of corporations upon the courts eventually led to an interpretation which went far to restrain the interference of state legislatures in the operation of business. To the rising capitalist and, in fact, to the average citizen, it seemed not only unnecessary, but bad economics, to regulate private capital. Capital should be aided, not impeded, in the development of the vast natural resources of which, it was believed, there was a sufficiency for all — a theory that was given practical application through the control of the federal government by the business interests during most of the period after 1860. This point of view was further strengthened by the pioneer individualism of a frontier people who demanded the utmost freedom of action. As a consequence, competition and *laissez faire* were the order of the day. These were the years when millions of acres were given to the railroads and charters bestowed with a free hand. The most valuable of the oil, lumber, and metal lands were occupied under federal land Acts, bought in, or obtained by fraud. Although there was indeed plenty for all, victory went to the strongest and the most unscrupulous. The same was true in the struggle for markets. The home market, which had been freely supplied with manufactured goods from abroad during the early decades of the century, was buying 89 per cent of its manufactured commodities from domestic producers by 1860, and 97 per cent by 1900. In the struggle for these resources and markets legislatures were bribed, the people robbed,[2] all sorts of illegal methods used, and even armed force resorted to upon occasion. As late as 1910 a well-known British journalist aptly likened the United States to "an enormously rich country

[1] "No State shall make or enforce any law which shall abridge the privileges or immunities of citizens of the United States; nor shall any State deprive any person of life, liberty, or property without due process of law; nor deny to any person within its jurisdiction the equal protection of the laws."

[2] M. N. Orfield, *Federal Land Grants to the States with Special Reference to Minnesota*, Bulletin of the University of Minnesota (1915), shows how the public lands, forests, and mineral wealth of one richly endowed state passed into private hands.

From *American Economic History* by Harold Underwood Faulkner. Harper and Brothers, 1949. Reprinted by permission.

overrun by a horde of robber barons, and very inadequately policed by the central government and by certain local vigilant societies."[3]

In a famous passage written in 1776, Adam Smith made the assertion: "Every individual is continually exerting himself to find out the most advantageous employment for whatever capital he can command. It is his own advantage, indeed, and not that of society, which he has in view. But the study of his own advantage naturally, or rather necessarily, leads him to prefer that employment which is most advantageous to society."[4] This roseate prediction made at the dawn of the Industrial Revolution as to the beneficial results of *laissez faire* upon the welfare of society was hardly borne out in the decades following the Civil War. Unbridled competition as it developed not only destroyed many manufacturers but in the end brought consolidation which often worked harm both to producers of raw materials and to consumers. With unrestrained competition and *laissez faire*, however, came evils which to a certain extent applied their own curb. The public reacted against the wasteful exploitation of the country's resources and the illegal methods so commonly used, and cutthroat competition was so disastrous that some way out had to be found. Business consolidation and government regulation have been the inevitable outcome.

Growth of Business Consolidation

The years before the Civil War saw the golden age of the small manufacturing business, the period when the typical

concern was owned by a single entrepreneur, a family, or a small handful of stockholders. Since the 'seventies the tendency has been to consolidate. Economists at opposite ends of the scale of economic thought have agreed that the consolidation of smaller units into larger is an inevitable result of the conditions brought about by the Industrial Revolution. Whether this trend is inevitable or not, it has without doubt been very marked in our economic life. Most of the witnesses appearing before the Industrial Commission in 1899 believed that "competition so vigorous that profits of nearly all competing establishments were destroyed"[5] was the chief motivating force for business combinations, and this appears to have been the immediate cause which led many to unite to escape being driven to the wall. The bitter rate wars of the railroads during the early 'seventies had driven fares and rates between competitive points below the cost of transportation. Competition was so excessive in the refining of sugar, for example, that eighteen out of about forty refineries had failed before consolidation was begun. Added to the losses from price cutting were the inherent losses of competition due to costs of advertising and salesmen, and the many disadvantages which a small industry must suffer in comparison with a large one in utilizing by-products, securing the best management, and bargaining with labor, bankers, and transportation companies. The desire to eliminate needless costs went hand in hand with the eagerness to reap greater profits, which were particularly available when the business, as in the case of the Standard Oil, was large enough to effect a monopoly.

[3] William Archer, "The American Cheap Magazine," *Fortnightly Review*, LXXXVII, 930 (1910).

[4] Adam Smith, *Wealth of Nations*, Book IV, Chap. II, fourth paragraph.

[5] *Preliminary Report of the Industrial Commission*, p. 9.

While these were the immediate causes, certain results of the Industrial Revolution made big business possible. The invention of labor-saving machinery made large-scale production profitable, the heavy fixed investment in expensive machinery and apparatus discouraged competition, and the very growth in the size of the nation and of its business tended, as in the case of the railroads, to inevitable consolidation. Gradually smaller inventions, such as the typewriter, adding machine, and many other appliances, contributed necessary elements to the age of big business. This development was greatly aided by the adoption of the corporate form, under which most large industrial units were organized. Likewise it should be remembered that concentration was a characteristic of the nineteenth century. It was to be seen not only in business, but also in labor in the formation of unions, and in the political world in the unification of Italy and Germany.

Laissez faire may have dominated American economic policy during the last half of the nineteenth century, but there was one notable exception to its sway. Under the influence of her developing industry the United States committed herself in 1861 to a system of high protective tariffs which in general she has maintained ever since. This deviation from *laissez faire* seems also to have aided in the development of big business and monopoly. Henry O. Havemeyer, president of the Sugar Trust at the time of its formation, asserted that "the tariff is the mother of trusts, and there were many who agreed. Although many monopolies, such as the Standard Oil Trust and the American Tobacco Trust, owed little or nothing to the tariff, there were others, like the Sugar Trust, that did.

In any event the tariff allowed monopoly profits.

"A calculation of the flat averages of the returns from all the leading industrial lines for which figures are given since 1850," assert Jenks and Clark, "gives almost startling demonstration of industrial concentration in the United States during the past two generations. Such a calculation shows that in thirteen leading lines of industry in the United States, the average manufacturing plant in the sixty years from 1850 to 1910 multiplied its capital by more than thirty-nine, its number of wage earners by nearly seven and the value of its output by more than nineteen."[6] This tendency continues to be an outstanding feature of American industry, as can be seen in the accompanying table. By 1923 the census had ceased to tabulate data for establishments whose annual output was less than $5000. From 1914 to 1929, small establishments doing a business of $5000 to $20,000 declined in relative numbers from 48.9 per cent to 32.9, while all the larger units increased; in percentage of wage earners these small units decreased from 6.0 to 2.3, and in value of products, from 3.7 to 1.1. It is interesting to compare these figures with those for establishments doing a business of one billion dollars or over, which showed enormous increases. Although in 1929 this class constituted only 5.6 per cent of the total, it employed 58.3 of the workers and produced 69.2 of the value of products.

Advantages and Disadvantages of the Corporate Form

As the size of the business unit increased and competition became more reckless and exacting, the old-fashioned

6 Jeremiah W. Jenks, and Walter E. Clark, *The Trust Problem* (7th ed., 1917), p. 17.

methods of conducting a business by means of individual ownership or partnership became inadequate. The funds needed for buildings, equipment, and

stocks were too great for individuals to supply, and the risk was too great to be undertaken singly. As a consequence, the corporate form of business was

Manufactures: Establishments Classified by Value of Products 1914–1929[7]

CLASS OF ESTABLISHMENTS ACCORDING TO VALUE OF PRODUCTS	ESTABLISHMENTS		WAGE EARNERS		VALUE OF PRODUCTS	
	NUMBER	PER CENT DISTRIBUTION	AVERAGE NUMBER	PER CENT DISTRIBUTION	AMOUNT	PER CENT DISTRIBUTION
$5,000 and over[a]						
1929	210,959	100.0	8,838,743	100.0	$70,434,863,443	100.0
1925	187,390	100.0	8,384,261	100.0	62,713,713,730	100.0
1921	196,267	100.0	6,946,570	99.4[a]	43,653,282,833	99.7[a]
1919	214,383	100.0	9,000,059	99.5[a]	62,041,795,316	99.8[a]
1914	177,110	100.0	6,896,190	98.2[a]	23,987,860,617	99.1[a]
$5,000 to $20,000						
1929	69,423	32.0	202,958	2.3	771,417,436	1.1
1925	55,876	29.8	156,373	1.9	628,373,403	1.0
1921	71,075	36.2	224,852	3.2	782,977,433	1.8
1919	79,699	37.2	227,977	2.5	866,086,290	1.4
1914	86,587	48.9	423,829	6.0	893,459,166	3.7
$20,000 to $100,000						
1929	75,225	35.7	693,155	7.8	3,587,697,276	5.1
1925	68,951	36.8	660,309	7.9	3,272,196,872	5.0
1921	72,251	36.8	746,024	10.0	3,330,350,409	7.6
1919	75,627	35.3	773,701	8.6	3,487,756,280	5.6
1914	56,557	31.9	995,743	14.2	2,540,949,405	10.5
$100,000 to $500,000						
1929	44,153	20.9	1,672,983	18.9	10,023,771,653	14.2
1925	42,209	22.5	1,675,911	20.0	9,576,090,022	15.3
1921	38,027	19.4	1,629,573	23.3	8,405,758,540	19.2
1919	39,477	18.4	1,712,854	18.9	8,929,364,110	14.4
1914[b]	30,147	17.0	3,000,612	42.7	8,759,391,117	36.2
$500,000 to $1,000,000						
1929	10,395	4.9	1,121,547	12.7	7,294,860,945	10.4
1925	9,771	5.2	1,131,439	13.5	6,870,112,293	11.0
1921	7,581	3.9	966,559	13.8	5,296,720,583	12.1
1919	9,197	4.2	1,112,815	12.3	6,457,485,019	10.4
1914[b]						
$1,000,000 and over						
1929	11,763	5.6	5,148,100	58.3	48,757,116,133	69.2
1925	10,583	5.7	4,760,229	56.7	42,366,941,140	67.5
1921	7,333	3.7	3,379,562	48.4	25,837,475,868	59.0
1919	10,413	4.9	5,172,712	57.2	42,301,103,617	68.0
1914	3,819	2.2	2,476,006	35.3	11,794,060,929	48.7

[a] Small percentages for establishments doing a business less than $5000 omitted.
[b] Figures include data for two groups, $100,000 to $1,000,000.
[7] *Statistical Abstract, 1933*, p. 693.

adopted after the Civil War to suit the new needs. Before that time it was used chiefly in the formation of banks, the building of turnpikes and railroads, or the launching of some project necessary for the public good, perhaps of such magnitude that the risks had to be widely distributed. It was generally looked upon as a dangerous and undemocratic form associated with the idea of monopoly, and one to be carefully supervised. In New York, for example, state incorporation under general laws was not permitted until the constitution of 1846.

A corporation, according to an excellent definition, is "a voluntary autonomous association formed for the private advantage of its members, which acts with compulsory unity and is authorized by the state for the accomplishment of some public good."[8] In other words, a corporation is an organization or association created by law under a charter which authorizes it to do certain things. Although not a person, a corporation is an artificial being which like a person may carry on business, break the law, sue and be sued. It has many advantages which explain its almost universal adoption. (1) It makes easier the raising of large amounts of capital. Under the terms of the charter, corporations are allowed to capitalize their holdings and issue stock. This stock may be bought by many persons who often contribute comparatively small amounts to build up a great business. Thus the American Telephone and Telegraph Company boasts of over 700,000 stockholders, the General Motors Corporation of more than 400,000, and several companies of over 200,000.[9] A corporation may also borrow money and issue bonds, thus giving it access to large resources of capital. (2) By owning corporate stocks, many people may share in the development of the country and in the profits of the largest concerns often managed by men of great ability, without themselves contributing anything but money. (3) The risk of the stockholders is limited by the law of the state. (4) The shares may usually be bought and sold, thus allowing a person voluntarily to enter or leave a concern as his private interests dictate. (5) The corporation has great advantages in that it is not disrupted by the death or retirement of its members.

On the other hand, the corporate form has disadvantages. Where the number of stockholders is large and scattered, it is impossible for them to exercise any real control over their delegated agents, the directors elected at the annual meetings. The irresponsibility of the directors is accentuated by the legal attitude that a corporation is a separate legal person and that the directors are the agents of the corporation and not of the stockholders, thus making it useless for a stockholder or a minority to sue a director or his agents for loss incurred through fraud or negligence. The lack of control of the stockholders over their directors has often encouraged the latter to use their position to promote personal interests or to

---

[8] L. H. Haney, *Business Organization and Combination*, p. 82. A more famous definition is that of Chief Justice Marshall in the Dartmouth College case: "A corporation is an artificial being, invisible, intangible, and existing only in contemplation of law. Being the mere creature of law, it possesses only those properties which the charter of its creation confers upon it, either expressly, or as incidental to its very existence. . . . Among the most important are immortality, and, if the expression may be allowed, individuality; properties, by which a perpetual succession of many persons are considered as the same, and may act as a single individual." Dartmouth College *v.* Woodward, Vol. IV, Wheaton's Reports, 518, p. 636.

[9] These are figures for 1945.

indulge in speculative management, fraudulent promotions, and overcapitalization, which have in the end worked havoc to the stockholders, who are not inclined to inquire too closely as long as dividends are unimpaired. From the point of view of the investor the numerous stock and bond issues so common to corporations are confusing, and only an expert can work out their true valuation. From the broader outlook of public policy, corporations seem to promote monopoly, for stock ownership facilitates interlocking directorates and interlocking ownerships. Whatever its disadvantages may be, however, the corporation has become the dominant form of business organization today. Although in 1919 corporations numbered only 31.5 per cent of the total establishments, they employed 86 per cent of the wage earners and produced 87.7 per cent of the total value of the products.[10] There is plenty of evidence to show that their relative importance has increased during the last two decades.

Evolution of Concentration

While some large concerns have achieved their size by internal growth and natural expansion, many more have come to their present greatness through the consolidation of industries engaged in the production of similar commodities. Attempts like those of the salt producers in western Virginia after 1830 to restrict output and thus control prices had been made before the Civil War, but it was not until after the panic of 1873 that the movement toward consolidation became important. The periods through which the consolidation movement has passed can be divided roughly according to the

[10] *Abstract of the Census of Manufactures, 1919,* Table 195, p. 340. Classification according to ownership was omitted between 1919 and 1925.

forms which it has taken: (1) pools, (2) trusts, (3) holding companies, (4) amalgamations and mergers, and (5) "community of interest."

POOLS. — Pools appeared after the panic of 1873 and the movement continued until about 1887. A pool is an organization of business units whose members seek to control prices by apportioning the available business in some way. This form was especially popular among the railroads, for the bitter rivalry between competitive points was fast leading to ruin. Although forbidden in the Interstate Commerce Act of 1887, the practice was continued, especially in the South, where the transportation of cotton was for a long time apportioned and the freight rates fixed by common consent. In addition to traffic pools there have been "output" pools, illustrated by the agreement between the powder manufacturers in 1886 which sought to eliminate "ill-regulated and unauthorized competition" by mutual understanding in regard to output and price. Informal apportionment of business among different units of the same industry undoubtedly still persists to some extent. Another form of pool is that in which territory and market are allotted. A typical example was the agreement entered into in 1902 between the Imperial Tobaccoo Company of Great Britain and the American Tobacco Company, giving the former exclusive control of the British Isles, and the latter control of the United States, her colonies, and Cuba; a new corporation, the British-American Tobacco Company, Limited, was to handle the business in the rest of the world. A more recent marketing pool was made shortly after the First World War when the British Marconi Company and the Radio Corporation of America attempted to divide between them the radio business of the world. Still another type of pool occurs when a certain part of profits or income is deposited with a central body to be distributed later.

TRUSTS. — Pools in railroads were declared illegal in 1887 by the Interstate Commerce Act, and again in 1897 by the Supreme Court in the case against the Trans-Missouri Freight Association. Pooling was deserted beginning in 1887 in favor of a new form of understanding which appeared to be legal and at the same time much more efficient. From that year until 1897 the trust was the most favored form of combination. A trust is a form of organization in which the stockholders under a trust agreement deposit with a board of trustees a controlling portion of their stock and receive trust certificates in return. Unlike a pool this is no mere federation; it is an actual consolidation of interests. It is a case of using the old legal idea of a trusteeship to create a monopoly, and was introduced as early as 1879 and 1882 by the Standard Oil Company. This was followed by the formation in 1887 of the "'Whisky Trust" (Distillers' and Cattle Feeders' Trust), the "Sugar Trust" (Sugar Refineries Company), the "Lead Trust," the "Cotton-oil Trust" (1884) and by others in succeeding years. The trust form, which gave absolute power to the trustees, created a monopoly, opposition to which produced anti-trust laws on the part of various states in 1889 and later, and the Sherman Anti-trust Act on the part of the national government in 1890. The early prosecutions by the federal courts under the Sherman Act were generally unsuccessful, but the dissolution of the North River Sugar Refining Company by the New York Court of Appeals in 1890 and of the Standard Oil Trust by the Ohio courts in 1892 put a decided damper upon this method of

consolidation. Interestingly enough, these cases were decided on the grounds that the creation of a trust had violated rights granted in the charter and not on the grounds that monopolies had been created.[11] In any event the decisions were accepted by the corporations. Moreover, the panic of 1893 and the succeeding years of depression held up for the time being further aggressive moves toward consolidation.

HOLDING COMPANIES. — The anti-trust legislation led to the adoption of a new form of consolidation, namely, the holding company. This was the form used during the greatest period of business consolidation, the years from 1897 to 1904. A holding company is an organization created to dominate other corporations by owning or controlling a portion of their stocks. Although this device had been employed before this time by the Pennsylvania Company and the American Bell Telephone Company, it was now adopted rapidly, the Standard Oil, as with the trust form, again taking the lead. The movement toward the holding company was greatly facilitated by the complacent laws of a number of states, particularly New Jersey, West Virginia, Delaware, and Maine, which permitted the organization of pure finance corporations under a general statute allowing the widest powers to these corporations. Their obligations were so slight that merely the maintenance of a dummy office and the submission of a meager annual report complied with the law. New Jersey, because of her position, was able to outbid the other states, and the providing of head offices to which directors might journey from New York to hold their annual meetings became an important industry in Jersey

11 H. R. Seager and C. A. Gulick, Jr., *Trust and Corporation Problems* (1929), pp. 51–55.

City. Between 1897 and 1904 over $6,000,000,000 worth of securities were marketed; in 1897 alone, new corporations were organized with a nominal capital of $3,512,000,000, of which at least one-fourth was "water." In 1904 John Moody listed 318 greater or lesser industrial trusts representing consolidations of nearly 5300 distinct plants and capitalized at over seven billions, of which 236 (with five-sixths of the capital) had been incorporated since January 1, 1898, 170 of them under New Jersey law.[12] In fact, most of the great corporations of today were formed during those years, including what for many years was the greatest of them all — the United States Steel Corporation.

This huge holding company, with its eleven constituent companies, controlling some 170 subsidiary concerns, was the handiwork of J. P. Morgan and Elbert H. Gary and in a sense marked the climax of the trust movement. The underlying impetus for its organization was the bitter competition in the iron and steel business and Andrew Carnegie's threat of even keener warfare in the future. Carnegie, anxious to retire, finally succeeded in unloading his vast steel properties upon Morgan, who merged them with a number of steel concerns in which he was already interested, and certain others that were brought in, the whole constituting the United States Steel Corpora-

tion. The actual value of the tangible property of this new corporation was estimated by the Commissioner of Corporations at $682,000,000; yet it was capitalized at $1,402,846,000, of which $510,205,000 represented preferred stock, and $508,227,000 common.[13] Obviously all of the common stock and an appreciable share of the preferred represented "water," but so powerful and so successful was the enterprise that with the exception of three years it paid dividends on its common stock until 1932. From the point of view of promoters and original investors it has proved one of the most successful of the great consolidations.

Mere size, as many investors discovered, did not necessarily mean profits. Such consolidations as the International Mercantile Marine Company and the United States Shipbuilding Company[14] brought losses rather than gains, and the speed with which consolidation proceeded filled the market with what Morgan called "undigested securities." By 1904, most of the important industries had been consolidated to a greater or lesser extent, and for the time being there were few remaining fields to conquer. Furthermore, when the holding company constituted a monopoly its position was no safer than that of the trust. In 1904 the Roosevelt administration secured the conviction and dissolution of the Northern Securities Company, an organization formed to hold the stock of the three great railroads tapping the Northwest. The courts affirmed that while a holding company was legal under the laws of the

[12] John Moody, *The Truth About the Trusts* (1904), p. 486. Seven of the greater trusts which he lists — the Amalgamated Copper Company (1899), the American Sugar Refining Company (1891), the American Smelting and Refining Company (1899), the Consolidated Tobacco Company (1901), the Standard Oil Company (1899), the U. S. Steel Corporation (1901), and the International Mercantile Marine Company (1902) — boasted an aggregate capital of over $2,500,000,000; with a single exception they were all formed after 1898, and all were incorporated under New Jersey law.

[13] *Report of the Commissioner of Corporations on the Steel Industry* (1911), Part I, pp. xvii–xxiv; also in F. Flügel and H. U. Faulkner, *Readings in the Economic and Social History of the United States* (1929), pp. 566–573.

[14] H. R. Seager and C. A. Gulick, Jr., *Trust and Corporation Problems*, Chap. XII.

incorporating states, it was illegal when the obvious intent was to effect a monopoly. In the same tenor subsequent decisions dissolved the Standard Oil and American Tobacco holding companies.

MERGERS AND "COMMUNITY OF INTEREST." — The holding company is still the most significant type of corporate organization in the United States and in recent years it has been carried to new refinements by means of "voting trusts," investment trusts, and pyramided holding companies (below, pp. 610 ff.). Nevertheless, other methods of consolidation have supplemented it. Amalgamation and merger of the outright purchase of one organization by another is one method. Likewise anti-trust laws have stimulated new methods of achieving monopoly through "community of interest," usually through the purchase of stock by individuals, holding companies, corporations, investment trusts, or "voting trusts." One company can buy a sufficient quantity of another company's stock to make its influence felt, and representatives of one company may thus sit on another's board. True, the Clayton Act forbids interlocking directorates in competitive companies engaged in interstate business whose capital, surplus, and undivided profits aggregate more than $1,000,000; but even here the same persons, as stockholders, may exercise great influence through "dummy" directors. So extensive was the "community of interest" in the oil companies that the dissolution of the trust in 1892 and of the holding company in 1911 made practically no difference. The railroads have been under the questioning eye of the people for so long that they especially have resorted to consolidation through "community of interest." To such an extent has the purchase of stock been consummated between the railroads that it is comparatively easy to divide them into eight or ten different groups according to their controlling financial interests, a situation which has almost eliminated competition in the sections served by these systems.

The Standard Oil Company

The history of the oil business is of particular significance in the study of industrial combinations, for the rise and progress of the Standard Oil Company illustrates practically every phase in the development and methods of monopoly under American conditions. Successful drilling for oil commenced in 1859 in the vicinity of Titusville, Pennsylvania, after the discovery of the Drake well. While the business of drilling wells and refining oil expanded rapidly during the war, the production in 1865 was behind the demand and the whole industry was severely handicapped by lack of transportation facilities and efficient refining machinery. The fact that transportation was the great problem and the chief expense of the expanding oil industry made it quite evident to the most able men in the business that success would come to the large concern with enough capital to install the best machinery for large-scale production and sufficient output to force favorable railroad rates. In 1867, while the industry was still in its infancy, John D. Rockefeller united the refineries of William Rockefeller & Co., Rockefeller and Andrews, Rockefeller & Co., S. V. Harkness, and H. M. Flagler into the firm of Rockefeller, Andrews & Flagler. "The cause leading to its formation," he said, "was the desire to unite our skill and capital in order to carry on a business of some magnitude and importance in place of the small business that each separately had theretofore carried on."[15]

15 *Preliminary Report of the Industrial Commission*, p. 95.

Further capital was needed, and in 1870 the company was reorganized into the Standard Oil Company of Ohio, with a capital of $1,000,000 and a refining capacity in its Cleveland plant of about 600 barrels a day. This amounted, however, to only 4 per cent of the oil refined in the United States, and the Standard plant was not even then the largest in the country.

Up to 1879 competition among oil men had been largely in production. In the succeeding years it was a competition for transportation facilities and favorable rates, a bitter war which left the Standard Oil Company in complete control. This victory may be attributed largely to the business acumen of Rockefeller and his associates, to favorable freight rates, and to the unscrupulous and illegal methods to which these men resorted to destroy competition and win favorable concessions from railroads and legislatures. Their desire to secure cheap transportation rates was aided by the railroads (chiefly the Erie, the New York Central, and the Pennsylvania, which were in competition for the oil business); in keeping with the policy of the time, the roads lowered their rates at competitive points and to promising concerns. In all the dickering with the railroads, no group of refiners was so successful as Standard Oil. Its favorable location at Cleveland was, to be sure, a factor in this success, since it freed the concern from complete dependence on the railroads by affording water transportation to the seaboard by way of the Great Lakes.

The most notorious of the rate agreements was made through the South Improvement Company chartered by the Pennsylvania legislature in 1871 with the widest powers, including authority "to construct and operate any work, or works, public or private, designed to include, increase, facilitate, or develop trade, travel, or the transportation of freight, livestock, passengers, or any traffic by land or water, from or to any part of the United States."[16] This company, 900 of whose 2000 shares were held by Rockefeller and his close associates, made contracts with the Pennsylvania, the New York Central, and the Erie, whereby it agreed to ship 45 per cent of all the oil transported by it over the first-named railroad and to divide the remainder between the other two roads. In return the railroads agreed to allow rebates on all petroleum shipped by the company and to charge all others the full rates, and in addition to furnish the South Improvement Company waybills of all petroleum and its products transported over their lines. Each road also agreed "at all times to cooperate, as far as it legally may, with the party hereto of the first part against loss by injury or competition, to the end that the party hereto of the first part may keep up a remunerative, and so a full and regular business, and to that end shall lower or raise the gross rates of transportation over its railroads and connections, as far as it legally may, for such times and to such extent as may be necessary to overcome such competition." The South Improvement Company aroused such a storm of opposition that its charter was revoked after three months, but, nevertheless, rebates and favorable discriminations were continued. The Standard Oil gradually extended its operations to include the ownership of pipe lines; by 1879 it controlled from 90 to 95 per cent of the oil refined and was able in turn to dictate its rates to the roads. The "Hepburn Committee," reporting to the New York legislature in January, 1880, said:

[16] *Ibid.*, p. 608. The charter of the South Improvement Company is given on p. 607, and the contract with the Pennsylvania on p. 610.

It owns and controls the pipe lines of the producing regions that connect with the railroads. It controls both ends of these roads. It ships 95 per cent of all oil. . . . It dictates terms and rates to the railroads. It has bought out and frozen out refiners all over the country. By means of the superior facilities for transportation which it thus possessed, it could overbid in the producing regions and undersell in the markets of the world. Thus it has gone on buying out and freezing out all opposition, until it has absorbed and monopolized this great traffic, this great production which ranks second on the list of exports of our country. The parties whom they have driven to the wall have had ample capital, and equal ability in the prosecution of their business in all things save their ability to acquire facilities for transportation.[17]

In order to dominate the situation more completely, the Standard Oil Company of Ohio worked out a scheme in 1882 by which the stock holdings of fourteen companies and the majority of holdings in twenty-six others were placed in the hands of nine trustees having irrevocable powers of attorney. The stockholders received trust certificates in return. The par value of these certificates amounted to $70,000,000, of which $46,000,000 was owned by the nine trustees who dictated the policies of the constituent companies. The public in general had no difficulty in understanding the purpose of this new organization. A wave of state anti-monopoly legislation followed and the courts of Ohio in 1890 broke up the Standard Oil Trust into twenty constituent companies. Trust certificates were replaced by proportionate shares of stock in the new companies.

In 1899 a second attempt was made to bring the entire properties under single control by the formation of the Standard Oil Company of New Jersey, a holding company as well as an operating company, formed with the intention of transferring to it the stock of the different corporations so that in time one concern might own and direct the whole industry. The new company's position as a holding company was gravely imperiled by the decision in the Northern Securities case (1904)[18] and was finally made untenable by the Supreme Court order of dissolution in 1911.[19] The business since then has been carried on by corporations chartered by the several states, which usually act harmoniously and exercise a dominant influence through a "community of interest" brought about by the ownership by certain individuals of controlling stock in the several companies. By 1904 Standard Oil controlled about 85 per cent of the domestic and 90 per cent of the export trade. Its earning capacity had increased from $8,000,000 in 1882 to $57,459,356 in 1905, and dividends from 5¼ per cent in 1882 to 30 per cent in 1898. In recent years the company has stretched into foreign fields, notably in Latin America, Rumania, and the Middle East. Increased motor traffic has added impetus to production and stimulated the formation of many new and powerful companies, such as the Texas, the Gulf, and the Shell Companies, which have effectively undermined the almost complete monopoly enjoyed forty years ago by the Standard Oil groups. The latter, however, continue to be dominant in the transportation and refining of oil and still far overshadow their rivals.[20]

[17] New York Assembly Document No. 38, 1880.

[18] Below, p. 18.

[19] Below, p. 18.

[20] For a brief review of Standard Oil history, see H. R. Seager and C. A. Gulick, Jr., *Trust and Corporation Problems*, Chaps. VI and VII, and H. W. Laidler, *Concentration of Control in American Industry*, Chap. II.

Combinations and Monopolies

The discussion so far has been largely concerned with the combination movement and the various forms it has taken. It should be remembered, however, that a pool, a holding company, or even a trust may be organized without effecting a monopoly. But the desire for a monopoly and its advantages has ordinarily been in the minds of the organizers, for a virtual monopoly may be brought about by controlling an important percentage of the product. So obvious was it that the trusts were organized to eliminate competition and to control products that the term "trust" has been commonly used in America to designate any large combination which approaches a monopoly, and it is sometimes even applied indiscriminately to any big business.

There are a number of different kinds of monopolies with which we are familiar. There may be *personal* monopolies in which an individual possessing special talent or knowledge may be able to drive out competitors. There are *legal* monopolies: public, such as the post office in America, or private, such as those based on patents, copyrights, or franchises. Another important group is the *natural* monopoly of situation or organization, as illustrated by a street railway, gas works, or anthracite coal mines. *Labor* monopolies resulting from combinations of skilled laborers often control the labor supply. But of special interest to us here are the *capitalist* monopolies or monopolies of organization which, by the concentration of large aggregations of capital and the unification of a sufficient number of production units, have been able to exercise a monopoly.

Even a cursory consideration of these types brings home the fact that certain forms of monopoly are inevitable and that others are encouraged for the sake of the public welfare. Personal talent or a steam railway is often an inevitable monopoly. A government post office system and a franchise creating a street railway may be monopolies established for the public good; broad social welfare is considered in the granting of patents. On the other hand, capitalist monopolies and monopolies of labor lead at once into controversial fields. But even here modern conditions prevent us from taking too dogmatic an attitude. The cost of erecting a sugar refinery or a steel mill is so great that free competition is almost automatically cut off, and labor's perfectly laudable determination to secure better conditions through a stronger bargaining organization cannot be condemned too hastily.

Capitalist Monopolies — Advantages and Disadvantages

Large-scale monopolistic production has always had its strong advocates as well as its critics. The former have emphasized in particular the savings in both production and marketing. As to production, they hold that the large resources make it possible to use only the best-located plants and the most efficient machinery, especially in slack times; that large-scale production allows more complete utilization of by-products and economies in the division of labor; that it permits the specialization of production at the different plants; that administrative expenses can be saved by the elimination of duplicated high-salaried positions and at the same time the best talent in the field can be secured; that research can be pursued on a larger scale; that waste and ineffective methods can be more easily detected through careful comparison of different plants that produce the same article; and that there is greater strength in dealing with labor.

As to marketing, it is maintained that expenses are reduced by the elimination of salesmen and advertising, by the elimination of cross-freights, since orders can be filled from the nearest plants, and by the development of greater strength in the export business. The argument is also advanced that control of the market price of both a raw commodity and the finished article helps to stabilize prices and production and thus exerts a healthy influence upon economic life. During periods of rapid monopolistic development, the evils of competition were always emphasized and the motto "competition is the death of trade" was kept well to the front.[21]

On the other hand, it is argued that while a monopoly may manufacture more cheaply, the savings are not passed on to the consumer, for a monopoly is usually formed to enhance profits, and there is conclusive evidence that in many cases the public has been gouged by unwarranted charges. It was the belief of the Industrial Commission in 1902, after a most exhaustive study, "that in most cases the combination has exerted an appreciable power over prices and in practically all cases it has increased the margin between raw materials and finished products. Since there is reason to believe that the cost of production over a period of years has lessened, the conclusion is inevitable that the combinations have been able to increase their profits."[22] A little earlier, Professor Jenks had come to the conclusion that "the fact that the power to increase the margin temporarily at least, somewhat arbitrarily, and the fact

that the margin has been increased in specific cases, seems to be clearly established."[23] While the price to the consumer has often been raised, the producers of the raw materials, such as cattlemen, sugar raisers, and others, have suffered from the lack of competition among buyers. Furthermore, monopoly has often resulted in inefficient and careless service to the consumer, and he has been forced to accept what was given him. Whatever might be the gains of monopoly from a purely scientific point of view, it was quite obvious that both the producer of the raw material and the consumer of the finished product were pretty much at the mercy of the manufacturer if the manufacturing processes constituted a monopoly.

In a comparison of the advantages and disadvantages, it should be pointed out that many of the alleged advantages of monopolies are similarly applicable to any large-scale industry where there is no monopoly. Steady consolidation of business has gone far, and there is every reason to believe that in most industries the process will continue. Nevertheless, monopoly as such has generally been distrusted as both an economic and a social evil, and persistent efforts either to restore competition or to control the inevitable monopolies have been undertaken through legislative means.

Early Anti-trust Movement

Notwithstanding the dominance of *laissez faire* and the enthusiasm with which business consolidation proceeded, there developed a strong opposition to the movement. This came first from the deep-seated antipathy to monopoly inherited from the old English common-

21 A. J. Eddy, the leading proponent of trade associations, epitomized this by the caption, "Competition is War, and 'War is Hell,' " across the title page of his book, *The New Competition* (1914).

22 *Final Report of the Industrial Commission,* XIX, 621.

23 Jeremiah W. Jenks, *Trusts and Industrial Combinations,* Department of Labor Bulletin, No. 29, July, 1900, p. 765.

law conception, a dislike which was undoubtedly stimulated by the misfortunes of those whose means of livelihood were injured by the new consolidations. Second, there was fear that the country's natural resources would be brought under the control of a few irresponsible men. By 1873 six corporations owned most of the anthracite coal deposits of Pennsylvania and the transportation facilities to carry the coal out, and in the succeeding years much of the bituminous field was appropriated. By 1882 thirty-nine refineries of the Standard Oil controlled 90 per cent of the product. "A small number of men," said Henry Demarest Lloyd (1894), "are obtaining the power to forbid any but themselves to supply the people with fire in nearly every form known to modern life and industry, from matches to locomotives and electricity. They control our hard coal and much of the soft, and stoves, furnaces, and steam and hot-water heaters; the governors on steam boilers and the boilers; gas and gas-fixtures, natural gas and gas-pipes, electric lighting, and all the appurtenances. You cannot free yourself by changing from electricity to gas, or from the gas of the city to the gas of the fields. If you fly from kerosene to candles, you are still under the ban."[24] By 1904 most of the great products of the country were in the control of big combinations, so large as to constitute monopolies.

Not only were the people disturbed over the appropriation and consolidation of the resources of the country, but they were thoroughly aroused over the dishonest methods of competition which in many cases had brought success by open evasion of the law. The concern that did not want to join the trust was throttled

by every unfair means known, among the least vicious of which was the obtaining of special railroad rebates, a practice which as much as anything else made possible the success of Standard Oil. Not only was there evasion of the law, there was tampering with the government; the unwholesome influence of big business upon politics was evidenced by the free distribution of railroad passes and still more by activities at election time. The supreme court of Michigan undoubtedly expressed the current feeling when it said in a case involving the Diamond Match Company, one of the most notorious of the trusts during the period: "Indeed, it is doubtful if free government can long exist in a country where such enormous amounts of money are allowed to be accumulated in the vaults of corporations, to be used at discretion in controlling the property and business of the country against the interest of the public and that of the people, for the personal gain and aggrandizement of a few individuals."[25]

Moreover, the financial practices incident to consolidation, the watering of stocks, the paying of enormous commissions to lawyers and banking houses, had helped to fleece the general public. And, finally, labor has found it more difficult to deal with the increased power of consolidated capital and has been among the severest critics of the trusts. Typical of this power was the United States Steel Corporation, which for more than thirty years prevented large-scale labor organization in its mills, and through its influence as the dominant concern in the industry also prevented organization in other companies.

This rapid growth of monopoly and the irresponsible use of the power which

24 H. D. Lloyd, *Wealth Against Commonwealth*, pp. 9–10.

25 Richardson *v.* Buhl *et al.*, 77 Michigan State Reports 658.

went with it were viewed with concern by many of the most thoughtful. Among the literature calling attention to defects in the economic life of the time, three widely read books stand out preeminently. Henry George in 1879 published his *Progress and Poverty*, in which he advocated a single tax on land values as one solution for the problem of monopoly. Edward Bellamy's *Looking Backward* (1887), by glorifying the socialist state, pointed to another solution; and Henry Demarest Lloyd's *Wealth Against Commonwealth* (1894) was the ablest and most effective attack ever delivered against trusts. The opposition which developed had already made itself felt in political channels. Further grants to railroad corporations and monopolies had been opposed by both the major parties in 1872. The Greenbackers in 1880 and the Anti-Monopolists in 1884 had called for government action to prevent or control monopolies, and this was true in 1888 of the platforms of the four leading parties — the Republican, Democratic, Prohibition, and Union Labor. Although monopolies were already presumably banned under the common law, twenty-seven states and territories by the close of 1890 had passed laws intended to prevent or destroy them, and fifteen states had incorporated provisions in their constitutions for the same purpose. In that year the federal government also took action.

The Sherman Anti-trust Act

By 1890 public opinion had become so aroused over the subject of monopolies that federal legislation was demanded to supplement state laws. Investigations undertaken in 1888 by a committee of the House of Representatives[26] and by

a committee of the Senate of the State of New York[27] offered little in the shape of constructive suggestion but confirmed current beliefs as to the evils of monopolies. President Harrison in his message of December, 1889, urged legislation against trusts which partook of the nature of conspiracies.[28] A number of anti-trust bills were introduced in the Senate in 1888, but two years of discussion ensued before a bill was eventually passed; its enactment was in no small measure due to the willingness of conservative Republican Senators to trade their votes to secure a simultaneous enactment of the McKinley tariff.

The Sherman Anti-trust Act of 1890[29] contained eight sections; the principle and theory of the Act, however, appear in the following:

Sec. 1. — Every contract, combination in the form of trust or otherwise, or conspiracy, in restraint of trade or commerce among the several States, or with foreign nations, is hereby declared to be illegal. . . .

Sec. 2. — Every person who shall monopolize or attempt to monopolize or combine or conspire with any other person or persons to monopolize any part of the trade or commerce among the several States, or with foreign nations, shall be deemed guilty of a misdemeanor. . . .

Fines and imprisonment were provided for violation, and the injured person

[26] *Report of Investigation of Trusts,* House Reports, 50th Cong., 1st Sess., 1887–88, Vol. IX, Serial Number 3112.

[27] *Report of the Senate Committee of General Laws on Investigation Relative to Trusts,* March 6, 1888.

[28] Richardson, *Messages and Papers of the Presidents,* IX, 43.

[29] 26 Stat. 209. The texts of this Act and the other federal anti-trust Acts mentioned in this chapter are to be found in Jeremiah W. Jenks and Walter E. Clark, *The Trust Problem,* in "Appendix F: Federal Trust Legislation in the United States." The various sections of the Appendix contain much valuable source material. See also F. Flügel and H. U. Faulkner, *Readings,* pp. 541 ff.

might recover three times the damages sustained. The several circuit courts of the United States were invested with jurisdiction to prevent or restrain violations of the Act, and the Attorney General was directed to institute proceedings in equity against such violations.

The Sherman Act was looked upon by many as an unnecessary blow at legitimate business and as futile opposition to an inevitable economic development. The committee who framed it maintained truly, however, that the bill was simply a restating of the usual English common-law principles and their extension to America. The Act did not attempt to define "contract, combination, or conspiracy in restraint of trade"; it was purposely drawn in general terms for the courts to interpret, the intention being that no business legitimately carried on need fear interference.

Senator Cullom called the Sherman Act "one of the most important enactments ever passed by Congress," but it was decidedly ineffective for a long while. This was due chiefly to three reasons — first, the economic depression in the succeeding years deferred further large-scale consolidation for some time; second, the general terms in which the bill was stated required much legal interpretation to be effective; and third, the federal government evinced lack of interest in enforcing it. The panic of 1893 temporarily crippled business and made both national and state governments loath to increase their burdens. The political weakness of the Harrison administration, followed by the necessary affiliations of Cleveland with eastern capitalists during his second term, prevented aggressive legislation; and under McKinley the combination movement went on merrily, with little apparent desire on the

part of the administration to interfere. Down to 1901 the government had instituted eighteen suits, but with discouraging lack of success. The spirit of *laissez faire* and the economic tendency during the period toward consolidation, combined with the difficulties of handling the technical questions involved in the trust and corporate form, hindered decisive and clear-cut judicial action. The futility of the Sherman Act seemed indisputable when in 1895 the Supreme Court refused to dissolve the American Sugar Refining Company (which had just acquired four competing Pennsylvania plants, thus enabling it to control over 95 per cent of the sugar refined) on the ground that the Sherman law was applicable only to monopoly in restraint of trade and that the mere purchase of sugar refineries or the refining of sugar was not commerce in the strict constitutional sense.[30] This almost incredible decision was considerably weakened, however, four years later in the Addyston Pipe case, when the Court held that, although the members of the pool manufactured pipe, their agreements were concerned with buying and selling across state lines, and in this case were illegal.[31] Although this case made it possible to accomplish something under the Sherman Act, we must agree with Professor Jenks when he says, "A study of these statutes and of the decisions of our courts of last resort which have been made under them will show that they have had comparatively little, practically no, effect, as regards the trend of our industrial development."[32]

[30] U. S. v. E. C. Knight Company, 156 U. S. 1.

[31] Addyston Pipe and Steel Co. v. U. S., 175 U. S. 211 (1899).

[32] J. W. Jenks, *The Trust Problem* (rev. ed., 1905), p. 218.

While the Sherman Act had little influence upon business consolidation, it is the irony of fate that capital had succeeded in using it effectively against labor unions. The Pullman strike of 1894 was broken by the government acting through the courts, when the latter held the actions of the union a conspiracy in restraint of interstate commerce and issued an injunction to desist.[33] In the famous Danbury hatters' case members of a labor union were held financially responsible under the Sherman Act to the full amount of their individual property for losses to business occasioned by an interstate boycott.[34] Certain courts actually went so far as to question the legality of trade unions *per se,* holding them, because of their restrictive rules and practices, as illegal combinations both at common law and under the Sherman Anti-trust Act.[35] In the Clayton Act of 1914, as we shall see, Congress tried to exempt labor unions from the application of the anti-trust Acts just as it tried more effectively to control business, but in neither case were its efforts crowned with notable success.

The Muckrakers and the Revival of Anti-trust Activities

The tremendous revival of the combination movement in the prosperous years immediately following the Spanish-American War, coincident with the abuses and the high-handed disregard of public welfare as evidenced by the

[33] *In re* Debs, 158 U. S. 564 (1894). See H. R. Seager and C. A. Gulick, Jr., *Trust and Corporation Problems,* pp. 374 ff.

[34] Loewe *v.* Lawlor, 235 U. S. 522 (1915).

[35] Kealy *v.* Faulkner, 18 Ohio Superior and Common Pleas Decision 498 (1908); Hitchman Coal and Coke Co. *v.* Mitchell, 202 Fed. 512 (1912).

large corporate interests, brought a logical reaction. Beginning with the publication in 1903–1904 of Ida M. Tarbell's "History of the Standard Oil Company" in *McClure's Magazine,* there ensued a period in which many of the worst features of our economic and social life were aired before the public. Lincoln Steffen's *Shame of the Cities* (1904) exposed the rottenness of many of the local governments; Thomas Lawson's "Frenzied Finance," published in *Everybody's Magazine* (1905–1906), showed Wall Street at its worst; Upton Sinclair in *The Jungle* (1906) revealed the horrible filth and misery of the workers in the meat-packing industry; Charles Edward Russell excoriated the "beef trust" in *Everybody's* in articles entitled "The Greatest Trust in the World"; Winston Churchill in *Coniston* (1906) drew a picture of the subservience of the state legislatures to the railroads; other phases of the railroad problems were handled by Ray Stannard Baker in a series, "The Railroads on Trial," in *McClure's;* and B. J. Hendrick in the same magazine laid bare the illegal and crooked practice of the insurance companies in "The Story of Life Insurance" (1907). Other books and numerous magazine articles enlarged upon the lawlessness and greed of big business and the venality of politicians. In the campaigns of 1896, 1900, and 1904 the Democrats directed part of their artillery against the trusts.

Some of this "muckraking" was undoubtedly exaggerated, but most of it, unfortunately, was only too true. Whether exaggerated or not, it helped to stimulate a healthy reaction for reform, a movement in which President Theodore Roosevelt took the lead. On a campaign speaking tour in 1902 he attacked the trusts, and in the next year

Congress passed three Acts to control big business more effectively. The first of these, known as the Expediting Act, gave preference to federal suits brought under the Interstate Commerce Act and the Sherman Anti-trust Act. The second was the Elkins Anti-rebate Act, which aimed to clarify the law and eliminate one of the worst practices of the railroads. The third created a Department of Commerce and Labor with a subsidiary Bureau of Corporations to make "diligent investigation into the organization, conduct, and management of corporations." In the same year the President directed his Attorney General to institute proceedings against the Northern Securities Company, a New Jersey holding corporation designed to create a transportation monopoly in the Northwest by controlling the stock of the Great Northern, the Northern Pacific, and the Chicago, Burlington, and Quincy. The successful issue of this suit[36] in 1904 showed that the Sherman Act might not be a useless reed in the hands of an aggressive administration. Under Roosevelt nineteen civil suits and twenty-five criminal suits were instituted in federal courts, and under Taft the effort to enforce the Sherman Act was carried on even more aggressively. The Pure Food Law of 1906 marked a distinct step forward in the policy of government intervention to protect the welfare of the public, while the more comprehensive Act of 1907 aimed especially to bring the meatpacking business under supervision.

Dissolution of the Standard Oil Company and the American Tobacco Company

The Taft administration believed that legitimate business might go on undisturbed and a solution to the trust problem be found by the voluntary federal incorporation of concerns, their charters to be approved by a projected corporation commission, with power reserved to Congress to revoke such charters. A bill to this effect was introduced, but public interest was never sufficient to push it through. As a consequence, the government continued to press the prosecutions already commenced, and succeeded in obtaining two notable decisions in 1911. The first of these, against the Standard Oil Company of New Jersey,[37] had been in the courts more than four years. The defendant argued that the Standard Oil companies were the natural products of the growth of a single business, that they had never competed with one another and consequently could not have conspired or combined in restraint of trade. Both the circuit and Supreme courts, however, affirmed the government's contention that the concerns had so conspired by many and devious methods to build up a monopoly. The dissolution was carried out by apportioning shares in the various constituent concerns pro rata to the stockholders of the holding company.

The case of the American Tobacco Company[38] was more complicated because the organization was not merely a holding company but an actual manufacturing concern, and one which was engaged in making a number of products, including chewing and smoking tobacco, snuff, little cigars, cigarettes, and tin foil. The court attempted to restore competition by creating separate companies in each line; for example, the manufacture of smoking tobacco was divided among

[36] Northern Securities Co., et al. v. U. S., 193 U. S. 360.

[37] U. S. v. Standard Oil Company of New Jersey et al., 152 Fed. Rep. 290; 173 Fed. Rep. 177; 221 U. S. 1.

[38] U. S. v. American Tobacco Co. et al., 164 Fed. Rep. 700; 221 U. S. 106.

four companies, cigarettes among three concerns, plug tobacco among four, and tin foil between two. A proportionate distribution of stock in the new companies was made, corresponding to the holdings in the old. Each new company was enjoined from cooperating with, or holding stock in, another company.

Two interesting facts stand out in regard to these decisions. The first is that the dissolutions failed in their purpose. In form there was competition, in reality there was little. The distribution of stock created simply a community of interest among the various concerns which appeared to work as harmoniously together as when under a single management. The increase in value of Standard Oil stocks after the dissolution showed that no detrimental results were feared. After more than thirty years of operation and numerous court dissolutions and interpretations, the Sherman Anti-trust Act appeared to have failed utterly in its purpose of preventing monopoly and restraint. The second point to be noted was the interpretation given to the Act by the two decisions. The Trans-Missouri Freight case decision (1897)[39] had refused to see any difference between reasonable and unreasonable combinations in restraint of trade, but the judges in the two decisions in 1911 professed to see a difference and maintained that the only restraint of trade which was intended by the law was that which monopolizes or attempts to monopolize. In other words, they introduced the so-called "rule of reason" and tried to differentiate between "good trusts" and "bad trusts." Many believed that the "rule of reason" was an unwarranted interpretation and that it simply weakened the Act. It certainly made further consideration of trust cases by the courts more complicated.

[39] U. S. *v.* Trans-Missouri Freight Association, 53 Fed. Rep. 440; 58 Fed. Rep. 58; 166 U. S. 290.

Eliot Jones: THE UNITED STATES STEEL CORPORATION: A Case Study

WITH the early history of the iron and steel industry we are not concerned. Even as late as 1890 there were practically no combinations of the modern type in the steel industry. To be sure, the Illinois Steel Company, for example, had been organized in 1889 as a consolidation of three erstwhile competitive concerns, yet such combinations were unusual. During the early nineties, however, the situation changed. The individual plants not only continued to expand in size, as during the eighties, but they became united in combinations. In 1891 the Lackawanna Iron and Steel Company was incorporated, a consolidation of the Lackawanna Iron and Coal Company and the Scranton Steel Com-

From *The Trust Problem in the United States* by Eliot Jones, copyright 1929 by Eliot Jones. Reprinted by permission of The Macmillan Company. [Because of the limitations of space all but the explanatory footnotes have been omitted from this selection. A student who wants to consult the source material should refer to the above book. Ed.]

pany. In 1892 the Colorado Fuel and Iron Company was organized to unite the Colorado Fuel Company and the Colorado Coal and Iron Company.[1] In the same year the Carnegie Steel Company (Ltd.), a partnership, was formed with a capital stock of $25,000,000. This concern, with all its plants concentrated at Pittsburgh, was then the largest in the industry. Yet it could hardly be considered a real combination, since it represented for the most part simply a more binding union of interests long affiliated. Other important concerns in the iron and steel industry in the early nineties were Jones and Laughlin; the Pennsylvania Steel Company, with its subsidiary, the Maryland Steel Company; the Tennessee Coal, Iron and Railroad Company; the Cambria Iron Company; and the Bethlehem Iron Company.

Most of the above enumerated concerns were engaged chiefly in the production of semi-finished steel (billets, blooms and slabs), and of the simpler and heavier forms of rolled steel products, such as rails, plates, and beams. The manufacture of the heavier steel products was concentrated to a considerable extent, even in the early nineties, in the hands of a comparatively few producers. Thus the Carnegie Steel Company, the Illinois Steel Company, the Jones and Laughlin interests, the Lackawanna Iron and Steel Company, the Pennsylvania Steel Company, the Cambria Iron Company, and the Bethlehem Iron Company together turned out nearly half of the steel ingots produced in this country (steel ingots are the raw material from which nearly all steel products are made, but they are generally put through a further process of

[1] The Colorado Fuel and Iron Company at this time, however, had a greater interest in the coal trade than in the iron and steel business.

manufacture before being sold). But these companies were entirely separate with respect to ownership, and in spite of the existence of pools of one kind or another were quite active competitors.

Save these companies producing the heavier steel products, there were comparatively few concerns of any considerable size in the iron and steel industry in the early nineties, and very few combinations. The Consolidated Steel and Wire Company, to be sure, was an important combination in the wire and nail business (1892), yet for the most part the manufacture of such products as nails, tin plate, and sheets was carried on by numerous concerns, many of them producing on a small scale. Competition in these lines was quite vigorous, except when restrained on occasion by pooling agreements.

The situation was the same in the iron mining industry. While there were a few large concerns, such as the Minnesota Iron Company and the Lake Superior Consolidated Iron Mines, organized in 1882 and 1893, respectively, yet in general the ownership of the iron ore mines was widely scattered; and though there were iron ore pools, competition was the characteristic feature of the industry.

In another respect the steel industry of the early nineties presented a marked contrast with the industry of today. This was in the comparative absence of integration, — the practice of uniting under one control the successive stages in the manufacture of the finished products. There was some integration, to be sure. The Carnegie Steel Company, for example, through the Frick Coke Company held large deposits of coking coal, and by the purchase in 1892 of a half-interest in the Oliver Iron Mining Company had provided itself with a supply of iron ore.

But the production of the Oliver concern was quite inadequate to the needs of the Carnegie Company, and moreover, Mr. Carnegie was understood to be opposed to the ownership of ore mines. The business of mining iron ore, like the production of crude oil, was largely speculative; and Mr. Carnegie, like Mr. Rockefeller, was willing that the risks be borne by those more speculatively inclined. Other companies had integrated their business slightly, yet generally speaking it was true that the manufacturers of finished products bought the semi-finished steel which constituted their raw material; the manufacturers of steel in turn bought their pig iron; and comparatively few iron and steel manufacturers possessed large iron ore deposits or iron ore railroads. The separate stages in the process of production were not at that time united under one management as at present.

From what has been said it is apparent that the leading characteristic of the iron and steel industry during the early and middle nineties was its competitive character. It is true that agreements were quite common; indeed, there was hardly any branch of the iron and steel industry that was free from them. Yet the pools generally maintained but a precarious existence, and this was especially true of the less formal "gentlemen's agreements."

In the latter part of the nineties, however, the situation underwent a marked change. In 1898 the combination movement struck the iron and steel industry, and by 1900 a large number of combinations had been formed. Some idea as to the extent of this movement is given by the following table, which shows the leading iron and steel combinations created during 1898 to 1900, with their authorized capitalization.

Leading Combinations in the Iron and Steel Industry, 1898–1900

A. COMBINATIONS LATER UNITED IN THE UNITED STATES STEEL CORPORATION

Name and year of organization	Capitalization
1898	
American Steel and Wire Co. of Illinois*	$ 24,000,000
Federal Steel Co.	230,217,179
American Tin Plate Co.	50,273,000
1899	
American Steel and Wire Co. of New Jersey	90,130,656
American Steel Hoop Co.	33,000,000
National Steel Co.	61,561,000
National Tube Co.	80,000,000
1900	
American Bridge Co.	70,156,000
American Sheet Steel Co.	54,000,000
Carnegie Co. of New Jersey	345,081,813
Shelby Steel Tube Co.	15,000,000
Total	$1,053,419,648

* This company was merged in 1899 into the American Steel and Wire Co. of New Jersey.

B. COMBINATIONS NOT SUBSEQUENTLY UNITED IN THE UNITED STATES STEEL CORPORATION

Name and year of organization	Capitalization
1898	
American Car and Foundry Co.	$ 60,000,000
American Iron and Steel Manufacturing Co.	20,000,000
Empire Steel and Iron Co.	10,000,000
National Enameling and Stamping Co.	30,600,000
Pressed Steel Car Co.	25,000,000
Republic Iron and Steel Co.	55,000,000
Sloss-Sheffield Steel and Iron Co.	23,835,000
United States Cast-Iron Pipe and Foundry Co.	30,000,000
Virginia Iron, Coal and Coke Co.	20,000,000
1900	
Crucible Steel Co. of America	50,000,000
Total	$ 324,435,000

In addition to these combinations there were a number of others in the machinery trade or similar branches of the industry. Among them were the American Bicycle Company, capitalized at $30,-000,000; the International Steam Pump Company ($27,500,000); the United

Shoe Machinery Company ($25,000,-000); the Otis Elevator Company ($11,-000,000); and the American Radiator Company ($10,000,000).

The first table shows the companies which subsequently united to form the United States Steel Corporation. A brief description of these companies will facilitate an understanding of the subsequent course of events.

Carnegie Company of New Jersey. The leading concern in the iron and steel industry, without a doubt, was the Carnegie Company of New Jersey. This company was organized in March, 1900, being simply a reorganization of the Carnegie interests and of the H. C. Frick Coke Company (owning extensive coking coal properties in the Connellsville district of Pennsylvania). It had an authorized capitalization of $320,000,000, half stock and half bonds.[2] All of its manufacturing properties were concentrated in the vicinity of Pittsburgh, thus giving compactness to its organization. The Carnegie Company also derived strength from the fact that its size had been attained largely through internal expansion, rather than through the acquisition of competitors, the purchase of the Duquesne works (1890) being the most important exception. The company was noted for its efficiency, its financial power, and its conservative management. It had built up its property chiefly out of earnings; its securities were not on the stock market; and its owners were actively engaged in the business. Among its more important subsidiary and allied concerns were the Oliver Iron Mining Company, the ore deposits of which, together with those secured by the lease of the properties of the Lake Superior Consolidated Iron Mines, assured the

[2] Not counting $25,081,813 of underlying indebtedness represented by bonds.

Carnegie Company an ample supply of good ore for a long time; the Pittsburg, Bessemer and Lake Erie Railroad, running from the Great Lakes to Pittsburg, and used mainly for the transportation of iron ore; the Union Railroad Company, operating an important belt line in the Pittsburgh district; and various gas, water, and dock companies.

The chief business of the Carnegie Company was the manufacture of semifinished steel for the trade, and of heavy steel products, such as rails, plates, structural steel, bars, skelp, and bridge material. Its leading position is indicated in the fact that in 1900 it produced some 18 per cent of all the ingots produced in the country, its nearest competitor producing only about 15 per cent. The Carnegie Company did not make such finished products as wire, nails, tubes, tin plate, and sheet steel; it merely supplied the manufacturers of these finished products with the necessary crude steel. But it was, nevertheless, in a position to turn out these finished products itself on comparatively short notice, should its customers decide to produce their own crude steel, — a circumstance that later proved to be one of the unsettling factors leading to the formation of the United States Steel Corporation.

The Federal Steel Company. The largest competitor of the Carnegie Company was the Federal Steel Company, organized in September, 1898. The Federal Steel Company was a consolidation of the Illinois Steel Company, with several steel plants in or near Chicago, and one at Milwaukee; the Lorain Steel Company, with a plant at Lorain, Ohio; the Johnson Company, with a plant at Johnstown, Pennsylvania; and the Minnesota Iron Company, which not only owned large iron ore deposits, but also an iron ore railroad from the mines to the Lakes (the Duluth and Iron Range Railroad), and a fleet of lake vessels by which the ore was carried from the railroad terminus to the lower lake ports. The Illinois Steel Company controlled the Chicago, Lake Shore and Eastern Railway, connecting its various plants in the vicinity of Chicago; and the Federal Steel Company itself acquired the stock of the Elgin, Joliet and Eastern Railway, a line connecting with nearly every railroad entering Chicago. The Federal Steel Company was thus well integrated; in fact, the chief purpose in its formation seems to have been not so much the suppression of competition as the creation of an organization that would be independently situated, not only with respect to its manufacturing plants, but also with respect to its ore, fuel, and means of transportation.

The Federal Steel Company, like the Carnegie Company, produced chiefly billets, steel rails, plates, structural shapes, wire rods, and semi-finished steel for the trade, many of its largest customers being themselves steel manufacturers. At the time of its organization in 1898 it produced about 15 per cent of the country's output of ingots, somewhat less therefore than the output of the Carnegie Company. The Federal Steel Company was generally rated as a Morgan property.

The National Steel Company. Next in importance after the Carnegie Company and the Federal Steel Company was the National Steel Company, organized in February, 1899. The National Steel Company was a consolidation of a number of steel concerns, located mainly in Ohio, and producing in 1899 about 12 per cent of the total output of steel ingots. It produced chiefly semi-finished steel, i.e., billets, sheet bars, and tin plate bars, rather than the finished products.

It had an excellent market for its crude steel through its close affiliation with the American Tin Plate Company, the American Steel Hoop Company, and the American Sheet Steel Company, all promoted by Judge W. H. Moore (the organizer of the National Steel Company), and all obtaining their raw material largely from it. The National Steel Company carried integration almost as far as the Carnegie Company and the Federal Steel Company, but differed from them in being also a combination of formerly competitive concerns.

The American Tin Plate Company — the tin plate trust. This company, organized in December, 1898, illustrates a group of combinations formed, not to integrate more fully the business of production (and thus to achieve a more strategic position), but to restrain or exclude competition. It brought together 39 plants, controlling 279 mills, which represented nearly every concern in the country making tin plate. It effected, therefore, a tin plate trust. Having done so, it attempted to strengthen its position by entering into exclusive contracts with the principal manufacturers of rolls and machinery used in the manufacture of tin plate, and thus to oppose an effective obstacle to the construction of competing mills. While this scheme was not altogether successful (the contracts were cancelled in 1902 at the insistence of the Steel Corporation), the company did succeed in maintaining for several years a monopolistic position in its branch of the steel industry.

The American Steel and Wire Company of New Jersey — the wire trust. This company represented another attempt to restrain competition and to make large promoters' profits. The dissolution of the wire nail pool toward the close of 1896 had been followed by marked reductions in prices, and this led to the organization in March, 1898, of a combination, — the American Steel and Wire Company of Illinois. The next year (January) the combination united with most of the remaining wire concerns to form the American Steel and Wire Company of New Jersey. This company produced mainly wire nails, plain wire, barbed wire, and wire fencing; and according to the brief for the government in its suit against the United States Steel Corporation it secured an almost complete monopoly of barbed wire and woven wire, and controlled about four-fifths of the nails and the wire fencing produced in the United States. The American Steel and Wire Company was well integrated, possessing, either at its organization or shortly thereafter, large ore deposits, a big reserve of coking coal, a large fleet of Lake vessels, and facilities for producing a limited amount of pig iron and crude steel.

The National Tube Company — the tube trust. The National Tube Company was incorporated in June, 1899, to monopolize the tubing industry, and incidentally to enable its promoters to make a profit through its organization (one-quarter of its $80,000,000 stock issue was given to the promoters). Its principal product was iron and steel wrought tubing, and the company stated in 1900 that its yearly capacity was 1,000,000 tons, or 90 per cent of the total capacity of the country. While this may have been an exaggeration of the extent of its control, nevertheless the company did produce nearly three-fourths of the country's output of wrought tubing. The National Tube Company, though rated as a Morgan concern, was largely dependent, because of the location of its plants, on the Carnegie Company for the semi-finished steel that constituted its raw material.

Subsequently it proposed to produce itself most of its raw material, with consequences soon to be described.

The American Steel Hoop Company. This company was formed in April, 1899. It united nine concerns producing mainly iron and steel bars, hoops and bands, cotton ties, and iron skelp. It was primarily a combination of erstwhile competitive concerns, and, according to the Commissioner of Corporations, a desire to limit competition and afford a large profit to the promoters was undoubtedly the ruling motive in its organization. The promoters received for their services $5,000,000 of the $33,000,000 stock issued by the company, or over 15 per cent of its total capitalization.

The American Sheet Steel Company — the sheet steel trust. This company was organized in March, 1900, to consolidate the properties of the principal manufacturers of sheet steel. Like the American Tin Plate Company it was formed to unite competing concerns; and it secured control upon its organization of about 70 per cent of the country's capacity of sheet steel, the only important product made by it.

The American Bridge Company. This company, like most of those already described, was organized (April, 1900), not to secure the advantages of integration, but the profits arising from a curbing of competition. Its main business was the erection of bridges and of steel construction for buildings, and it was entirely dependent on the large steel manufacturers for its raw material. The American Bridge Company, like the Federal Steel Company and the National Tube Company, had close affiliations with the firm of J. P. Morgan and Company.

The Shelby Steel Tube Company — the seamless tube trust. This company, incorporated in February, 1900, combined practically all the concerns in the country manufacturing seamless tubing. It claimed 90 per cent of the country's output, and there is no doubt that it did have a substantial monopoly of its special product until its field was invaded by the National Tube Company. The motive in its organization was the establishment of a trust; the element of integration was distinctly lacking.

The Lake Superior Consolidated Iron Mines. The combinations and trusts just described were all organized between 1898 and 1900, and each of them became a part of the United States Steel Corporation. One other concern, organized somewhat earlier, deserves mention. The Lake Superior Consolidated Iron Mines, largely owned by Standard Oil interests, was organized in 1893. It manufactured no iron or steel; it was simply an ore producer and a transportation company. It had vast reserves of iron ore, and it owned an important iron ore railroad, — the Duluth, Missabe and Northern. Affiliated with it was the Bessemer Steamship Company, the largest owner of ore vessels on the Great Lakes. The Lake Superior Consolidated Iron Mines, both because of its property and its financial backers, was a very important concern, and its acquisition by the United States Steel Corporation in 1901 greatly strengthened the latter's position.

What is the explanation of this remarkable movement toward combination in the iron and steel industry? The advantages which these combinations might have expected to gain were three-fold: (1) the restriction of competition; (2) a greater degree of integration; (3) stock market profits for the promoters.

The large profits that the manufacturers hoped to gain were realized. Aided by the favorable industrial situation,

these combinations and trusts were able to put prices up to very high figures. The price of Bessemer pig iron, which had averaged $10.32 per gross ton in 1898, went up to $18.88 per ton in 1899, and to $24.72 in March, 1900. The price of steel billets had been $15.18 per gross ton in 1898; it rose to $29.81 per ton in 1899, and to $33.00 in March, 1900. The price of steel rails averaged $17.63 per gross ton in 1898, $28.13 in 1899, and $35.00 in March, 1900. The price of tin plate averaged $64.08 per gross ton in 1898; the next year it went to $95.48. Prior to the formation of the tube trust the price of tubes had been $30.00 per ton. During 1899 (the year of its formation) the price rose to $67 per gross ton, and early in 1900 reached its maximum at $89. Further details may be had by consulting the table. It is not meant to imply, of course, that all of these price advances were the result of the formation of combinations and trusts; but it is safe to say that they took full advantage of the favorable industrial situation.

AVERAGE PRICES OF CERTAIN IRON AND
STEEL PRODUCTS IN 1898, 1899, AND
MARCH AND OCTOBER, 1900

Commodity	Per gross ton			
			March,	October,
	1898	1899	1900	1900
Pig iron*	$10.32	$18.88	$24.72	$13.06
Billets*	15.18	29.81	33.00	16.50
Rails†	17.63	28.13	35.00	26.00
Plates*	24.23	49.36	45.25	24.19
Structural shapes (beams)*	26.25	40.49	50.40	33.60
Tin plates‡	64.08	95.48	108.42	93.86
Wire nails*	29.91	52.04	71.68	49.28
Bars*	21.32	41.36	50.40	24.42
Sheets (black)*	42.28	60.24	67.20	62.72

* F.o.b. Pittsburg.
† F.o.b. Pennsylvania manufacturing plants.
‡ F.o.b. New York.

The desire to restrict or eliminate competition was, according to the Commissioner of Corporations, undoubtedly the main reason for the formation of these combinations. Taken as a whole, the iron and steel manufacturers had been very prosperous, but the severe industrial depression which began in 1893 and lasted until 1897 had cut into their profits heavily.[3] The manufacturers were anxious to restore the palmy days, and therefore turned to combination and monopoly as likely to prove more effective than pools, which were not only industrially unstable, but illegal as well.

A second advantage in combination lay in the possibilities of integration. A company which combined under one management the successive stages in the productive process was able to effect certain economies that were not open to a nonintegrated concern. These economies included a saving in fuel costs (those connected with the reheating of the metal), a saving in the labor and time involved in moving the materials, and the utilization of by-products, especially blast furnace gas. These particular economies, of course, could be availed of only by a vertical combination (an integrated concern); a horizontal combination (a combination of plants making substantially the same product) must justify itself, if at all, on other grounds; must point to other economies than those mentioned. On this phase of the matter more will be said later, but we may note at this point the necessity of keeping clearly in mind the distinction between the economies in producing and selling that were attainable by such of these combinations as did not possess monopolistic power (the Carnegie Company, the Federal Steel Company, and the National Steel Company, for example), and the additional economies that might be

[3] The competition between the steel manufacturers was not "ruinous."

secured through the organization of a trust (with monopolistic power), as, for example, the American Tin Plate Company, the American Steel and Wire Company, and the National Tube Company. The economies permitted by integration were notable, and no doubt combinations formed to realize them were in the public interest. Yet, as we have seen, a number of these early steel combinations were not vertical combinations, but horizontal combinations. They were not organized for the purpose of securing the advantages of integration, but the profits of monopoly. As the Circuit Court said: "Properties were assembled and combined with less regard to their importance as integral parts of an integral whole than to the advantages expected from the elimination of the competition which theretofore existed between them."

Another gain from integration was the possibility it offered of securing the profits which would otherwise go to the manufacturers or producers of the products at the earlier stages. Here was an opportunity to apply Mr. Rockefeller's maxim, "pay a profit to nobody." The gain was especially worth while because of the possibility that a pool or combination controlling the necessary raw material or semi-finished products might charge unreasonable prices. The company producing its own raw materials was assured an ample supply of them at cost to itself. With it companies not so well fortified could not compete advantageously.

The third advantage offered by the combination was the opportunity of making profits from the sale of the securities of the consolidated companies. The profits which were made in this way were of two kinds: first, those made by the manufacturers themselves; and, second, those made by the promoters. That the promoters had a direct financial inducement to form combinations and trusts is shown by the fact that the promoters of seven of these organizations (Federal Steel Company, National Steel Company, American Tin Plate Company, American Steel and Wire Company of New Jersey, National Tube Company, American Steel Hoop Company, American Bridge Company) received in the aggregate over $63,000,000 in stock as their pay. This was not all profit, to be sure, but to say that the compensation was very liberal is expressing it mildly. The profits were likely to be greater, of course, when the promoters were successful in establishing a trust than when they simply effected a combination possessing no monopolistic power. Some of these iron and steel combinations, as has been shown, belonged to one class; some, to another.

The underlying motive in the formation of the steel combinations and trusts of 1898–1900 was, as we have seen, the restriction or smothering of competition. Yet competition, though greatly restrained in several branches of the steel industry, was not destroyed. Indeed it soon appeared that the formation of these combinations was likely to lead to even more vigorous competition than ever. This unexpected outcome was the result of an attempt on the part of some of these combinations to integrate themselves so fully that they would be entirely independent of any other steel concern. To ward off the threatened competitive struggle, the United States Steel Corporation was formed. The circumstances leading up to its formation may be considered in some detail.

The combinations already described may be roughly divided into two groups: (1) the primary group, including the Carnegie Company, the Federal Steel Company, and the National Steel Company, concerns manufacturing chiefly semi-finished steel and the heavy steel products; (2) the secondary group, including the American Tin Plate Company, the American Steel and Wire Company, the National Tube Company, the American Steel Hoop Company, the American Sheet Steel Company, the American Bridge Company, and the Shelby Steel Tube Company, concerns manufacturing chiefly the lighter and more highly elaborated steel products. The companies in the secondary group were largely, some almost entirely, dependent on the primary group for the semi-finished steel which constituted their raw material; while the primary group, in turn, disposed of a large part of its output to the secondary group. There was thus a marked interdependence among the two groups, and for a while all went well.

This state of harmony, however, was not to endure. During 1900 the steel trade suffered a reaction, which made necessary the reduction of expenses, if returns large enough to pay dividends on watered stock were to be realized. Some of the concerns in the secondary group soon proposed therefore to integrate themselves still further, and thus to obtain their raw material at cost. The American Steel and Wire Company of New Jersey, for example, made plans to build additional blast furnaces and a large steel plant. The Carnegie Company and the Federal Steel Company, both of which had just enlarged their works, therefore faced the loss of a market for a considerable part of their output. To protect themselves, they decided to produce the more highly elaborated products, thus making use of nearly their entire semi-finished steel output and freeing themselves from their dependence on other steel manufacturers. In 1900 the Federal Steel Company proposed to undertake the manufacture of tubes and structural material. In the summer of 1900 it was reported that the Carnegie Company would engage on a large scale in the manufacture of wire rods. In January, 1901, the Carnegie Company announced that it proposed to build at Conneaut Harbor, Ohio, the largest pipe and tube plant in the world. The impression was current that the Carnegie Company would eventually make tin plate, sheet steel, and other finished products. The outcome of this policy of retaliation would clearly be two-fold: first, an increase in the country's productive capacity far beyond its normal consuming power; and, second, an abrupt termination of the monopolistic or semi-monopolistic position attained by the concerns in the secondary group.

A severe competitive struggle thus seemed imminent. And in such a struggle it was generally believed that the Carnegie Company would emerge the victor. This concern was credited with owning the best equipped and best managed steel plant in the country, if not in the world. In self-sufficiency of product it was well ahead of its rivals. In fact, there seems to have been little doubt that from the manufacturing standpoint the Carnegie Company would have proved more than a match for its competitors, many of whom, in their endeavor to monopolize the business, had been obliged to acquire at high prices numerous inferior plants. From the banking and financial standpoint the Carnegie Company was equally well fortified. It had ample capital and credit; and its securities were closely held, hence its owners were uninfluenced by stock market considerations. As Mr. Carnegie had remarked, the partners knew nothing

about the manufacture of bonds and stocks; they knew only about the manufacture of steel. The Morgan companies — the Federal Steel Company, the National Tube Company, and the American Bridge Company — naturally had excellent financial backing, but the Morgan financiers were tied up in other lines, particularly railroad enterprises, and they did not welcome a steel war. The Lake Superior Consolidated Iron Mines with Rockefeller support could, of course, have weathered any struggle, but this company was not engaged in steel manufacturing, and therefore was not directly concerned. The remaining companies, however, mostly Moore concerns, were very heavily overcapitalized, and had a highly speculative backing. The promoters of these companies had not yet had sufficient time to unload on the public, and so far as they were concerned a trade war had to be prevented at all hazards. Could the conflict be averted, the promoters could await a favorable opportunity for the disposal of the stocks held by them, and they might even realize some additional profits through the sale of the securities of the consolidated company on the rising market that would follow the restoration of harmonious relations.

The result of this situation was the formation of the present steel trust. On February 25, 1901, the United States Steel Corporation was incorporated under the laws of New Jersey (with an authorized capital stock of $3,000), in accordance with a plan to acquire the securities of the Carnegie Company, the Federal Steel Company, the National Steel Company, the American Tin Plate Company, the American Steel and Wire Company, the National Tube Company, the American Steel Hoop Company, and the American Sheet Steel Company. The

32591

offer of the Steel Corporation to exchange its securities for those of the companies named was promptly accepted by a great majority of the stockholders (over 98 per cent in each case); and therefore on April 1 the Corporation filed amended articles of incorporation whereunder its authorized capital stock was increased to $1,100,000,000. By this process of exchange (when completed) the Steel Corporation became strictly a holding company trust. Shortly thereafter it acquired the American Bridge Company, the Lake Superior Consolidated Iron Mines, the Bessemer Steamship Company, and the Shelby Steel Tube Company.

The restriction of competition was plainly the main motive for the formation of the Steel Corporation.[4] We should not be surprised, therefore, to learn that not only was the decline in prices then

AVERAGE PRICE OF CERTAIN IRON AND
STEEL PRODUCTS IN OCTOBER, 1900,
AND MAY, 1901

Commodity	Per gross ton	
	October, 1900	May, 1901
Pig iron*	$13.06	$16.30
Billets*	16.50	24.00
Rails†	26.00	28.00
Plates*	24.19	35.39
Structural shapes (beams)*	33.60	35.84
Tin plates‡	93.85	93.86
Wire nails*	49.28	51.52
Bars*	24.42	31.58
Sheets (black)*	62.72	71.68

* F.o.b. Pittsburg.
† F.o.b. Pennsylvania manufacturing plants.
‡ F.o.b. New York.

taking place arrested, but that prices were actually advanced. This is shown by the table above, giving the average

4 Judge Woolley in a separate opinion in the steel trust case said that his conclusions of fact and of law were that the *organizers* of the Corporation intended to create a monopoly and to restrain trade. 223 Fed. Rep. 178.

monthly price of certain iron and steel products in October, 1900 (just prior to the negotiations leading to the organization of the Steel Corporation), and their price in May, 1901, the first month after the organization of the Corporation.

Though the restriction of competition was the controlling motive in the organization of the Steel Corporation, at least two other influences were present. One was the desire to secure large profits through the sale of the securities of the new company. This matter is discussed in chapter XII; it will suffice here to point out that the underwriting syndicate realized a profit of $62,500,000 through the promotion of the Steel Corporation.

Another reason for the organization of the Steel Corporation was the desirability of integrating the business more fully, and of securing the economies of the trust form of organization. These two considerations, to repeat, must be sharply distinguished. Complete integration can be secured without resort to a trust, i.e., without attaining a monopolistic position at any stage in the process of production, whereas the economies of the trust form of organization can be secured, of course, only by a trust. The significant inquiry always is: can a trust produce more cheaply than a combination, more cheaply even than a highly integrated combination? If it can, anti-trust legislation is likely to prove futile. Now the organization of the Steel Corporation did lead to a somewhat greater degree of integration. The bringing together under one control of the iron ore mines, the iron ore railroads, the Lake vessels, the coking properties, and the plants making all kinds of iron and steel products meant that the Corporation was quite independent of others, and that no profits at any stage in the productive process need to be paid to anyone else. So far as the manufacturing processes were concerned, it is doubtful whether anything particular was gained; the advantages of integration were already about as fully realized by the larger and stronger of the constituent companies, such as the Carnegie Company, or if not already realized, would have been upon the completion of the extension proposed in 1900 to 1901.

As to the economies of the trust form of organization detailed information, as usual, is difficult, if not impossible, to secure.[5] It is probable that the steel trust, simply because it was a trust, did effect certain savings. The combining of so many manufacturing properties under one management probably made possible a more economical subdivision of the business whereby particular plants could specialize on certain products, with a consequent reduction in cost. The distribution of the Steel Corporation's plants also gave it an important advantage with respect to transportation costs; it could ship from the nearest mill, and thus save cross freights.[6] Savings were undoubt-

[5] The Bureau of Corporations in part III of its Report on the Steel Industry made a study of the cost of producing various steel products, but its investigation threw no light on the costs of the Steel Corporation as compared with the costs of other large and well integrated concerns. In fact, the Bureau, in order to protect the privacy of business, particularly refrained from giving any figures which would reveal the costs at the several independent plants.

[6] Mr. Schwab at a dinner held on December 12, 1900, discussed the advantages that might be derived from a combination, and referred specifically to specialization, location of plants near the centers of consumption, competition of the several managements, reduction in overhead expense, and the development of the export trade. He expressed the opinion that from a metallurgical or mechanical standpoint the limit of economies had been reached, or nearly so, so highly perfected had the processes of manufacture become.

edly effected through competition between the managers of the different plants; and a more complete utilization was made of certain by-products, such as blast furnace slag (used in the manufacture of cement), which was formerly a waste product. No doubt, also, the large capital possessed by the Steel Corporation assisted it in developing the export trade – claimed by the promoters to be one of the principal reasons for forming the Corporation – but it does not follow that the amount of capital required could have been supplied only by a trust. How important the above enumerated economies were it is not possible to say, but in view of the rapid growth of the independent concerns, as described later, it is not likely that they were controlling. Certainly few, if any, economies were achieved by the trust in the selling end; selling expenses in the iron and steel trade are a comparatively minor factor. In fact, the Commissioner of Corporations believes, the argument of economy in production was probably brought forward to justify the establishment of the trust, and to promote the sale of the company's securities; the main reason for the organization of the Steel Corporation was certainly the hope of averting the threatening competitive struggle.

The capitalization of the Steel Corporation was enormous. Under its amended certificate of incorporation it issued $304,000,000 of bonds, exclusive of $81,000,000 underlying indebtedness, and was authorized to issue $1,100,000,000 of stock, half preferred and half common. All of the bonds and $425,000,000 of each class of the stock were issued, mainly in exchange for the securities of the companies first acquired. Shortly after its organization the Corporation acquired the Lake Superior Consolidated Iron Mines and other concerns, and as a result its issue of each class of stock increased to over $500,000,000, making a total stock issue of over $1,000,000,000. The Steel Corporation, measured by capitalization, and perhaps by any test, was the largest industrial corporation the country had yet produced.

The company upon its organization controlled three-fifths of the steel business of the country. It produced almost 60 per cent of the pig iron used for steel making purposes, about 66 per cent of the crude steel output, and about 50 per cent of the finished steel products in the manufacture of which it was engaged. It had hundreds of millions of tons of iron ore; over 50,000 acres of the best coking coal lands; over 1,000 miles of railroad, including the iron ore railroads; more than one hundred Lake vessels; and large miscellaneous holdings, such as docks, natural gas and limestone properties. Yet despite its enormous size the Steel Corporation did not secure a monopoly of the iron and steel industry, though in certain lines its position was distinctly monopolistic.[7] This is indicated by the following table, showing the Steel Corporation's computation of its propor-

	PER CENT
Pig iron, spiegel and ferromanganese	43.2
Steel ingots and castings	65.7
Rails	59.8
Structural shapes	62.2
Plates and sheets	64.6
Black plate produced in tin mills	79.8
Coated tin-mill products	73.1
Black and coated sheets produced in tin mills	67.3
Wire rods	77.7
Wire nails	68.1
Wrought pipe and tubes	57.2
Seamless tubes	82.8

[7] That its position was not even more monopolistic in certain lines resulted from the fact that some of the constituent trusts had lost heavily in their percentage of the country's trade since their organization some two or three years previous.

tion of the country's output of the leading products in 1901.

Among the more important rivals of the Steel Corporation in 1901 were Jones and Laughlin, the Lackawanna Iron and Steel Company, the Republic Iron and Steel Company, the Pennsylvania Steel Company, the Cambria Steel Company, and the Bethlehem Steel Company. The Colorado Fuel and Iron Company because of its location was not an effective rival, though the Steel Corporation conducted negotiations looking toward its acquisition; and the Tennessee Coal, Iron and Railroad Company was at this time chiefly engaged in the production of foundry pig iron.

The capitalization of the Steel Corporation as noted above was enormous. But so was the amount of property acquired. Was the Corporation overcapitalized?

The capitalization of the company in 1901 after the acquisition of the Shelby Tube Company (in August) was as follows:

Steel Corporation bonds	$303,450,000
Underlying bonds	59,091,657
Purchase money obligations, etc.	21,872,023
Preferred stock	510,205,743
Common stock	508,227,394
Total	$1,402,846,817

The Bureau of Corporations made a detailed study of the value of the properties of the Steel Corporation in 1901 in order to determine whether the company was overcapitalized, and if so, to what extent. Three different methods were employed. The first method was an historical study, an analysis of the investment of the constituent companies at the time of their organization. The second method was a mathematical computation, a summation of the market value of the securities of the constituent companies, using the average weekly prices from the date of the organization of these combinations up to December 31, 1900. The market prices during the early months of 1901 were not included, since these were naturally influenced by the prospective organization of the Steel Corporation. This second method represented the estimate put by the public on the securities of the constituent companies, and it therefore reflected the probable earning power of these combinations. The third method was a physical valuation, a detailed estimate of the physical properties of the Steel Corporation by departments of its business, the valuation of the ore properties being made in particular detail. The valuation arrived at by the Bureau by the first method was $676,000,000; by the second method, which included intangible items, $793,000,000; and by the third and more accurate method, $682,000,000.

The conclusion of the Bureau, therefore, was that the entire issue of common stock was water, i.e., had no property back of it; and that a large amount, one-fifth to two-fifths, of the preferred stock was water. Even including the intangible assets, the common stock represented nothing but the hope of monopoly gains. By any reasonable standard, therefore, the Steel Corporation was very heavily overcapitalized.

After 1901, however, the Steel Corporation added greatly to its investment. This it did, first, by the construction of additional plants out of surplus earnings or out of the proceeds of issues of securities; and, second, by the acquisition of competing concerns through the sale of its own securities. The most important piece of new construction was the plant at Gary, Indiana, the largest steel plant in the world. This plant up to December, 1911, by which date practically all the construction then authorized had been completed, had cost over $62,000,000. Another new steel plant was built in Duluth, Minnesota, and a very large cement works was constructed in Buffington (near Chicago) by the Universal Portland Cement Company, a subsidiary of the Steel Corporation. Other important additions also were made by the Steel Corporation (through its subsidiaries).

The investment of the Steel Corporation has likewise been increased through the acquisition of competing companies. In 1902 the Steel Corporation purchased the Union Steel Company, which held large deposits of iron ore and coking coal; and in 1904 it acquired all the stock of the Clairton Steel Company, then in receiver's hands, but in the possession of important ore and coking coal lands.

But far more important was the purchase in November, 1907, of the Tennessee Coal, Iron and Railroad Company. This company, with its main plant located at Ensley, Alabama, was the most important iron and steel concern in the south. It produced 3 per cent of the country's output of iron ore, 2.9 per cent of the output of coke, 2.4 per cent of the pig iron, 1.1 per cent of the ingots and castings, and 4.3 per cent of the rails. Partly because of the fact that all the essential materials were assembled by nature within a radius of a few miles, the Tennessee Company was able to manufacture pig iron cheaper than it could be made in any other section of the United States. The company was controlled by powerful financial interests; and improvements were then under way to double its steel output and rail capacity. The Tennessee Company made open-hearth steel rails — in 1907 it produced 59.1 per cent of the total output of open-hearth rails — and was thus in a position to profit by the increasing demand for that type of rail. But the most important assets of the Tennessee Company were its enormous holdings of ore and coal; it owned more iron ore and coal adapted for making steel than any company in the United States except the Steel Corporation. There can be no doubt that the desire to secure these deposits had much to do with the purchase of the company. Moreover, the acquisition of the Tennessee Company made it impossible for it to effect a combination with the Republic Iron and Steel Company and the Sloss-Sheffield Steel and Iron Company, as had been planned, and thus to become an even more formidable competitor of the United States Steel Corporation.

The construction of new plants and the acquisition of competing plants greatly increased the investment of the Steel Corporation. This investment in 1901, as shown above, was $676,000,000. Between 1901 and the close of 1910 the investment increased by $504,928,653, of which amount about $435,000,000 was provided for out of surplus earnings.[8] By December 31, 1910, therefore, the total investment of the Steel Corporation amounted to $1,181,000,000. The capitalization of the company on the same date was $1,468,033,260, or about $287,000,000 in excess of the investment. In other words, about $287,000,000 of the Steel Corporation's stock was still "water." It is apparent that after 1901 the Corporation squeezed out a large part of the water in its stock. In 1901 the amount of water had been $726,000,000, using the actual investment as the basis of calculation, and $720,000,000, using the physical valuation as the basis. By 1910 the amount of water had been re-

[8] This increase in the investment was over and above a proper allowance for maintenance, repairs, and depreciation.

duced to $287,000,000 by the first method of calculation, and to $281,000,000 by the second. All of the water had been extracted from the preferred stock, and about half of the water from the common stock.

To have added so greatly to the value of its property, the earnings of the Steel Corporation must have been enormous. That they were so in fact is indicated by the table below, showing for the years 1901 to 1910 — the government dissolution suit was brought in 1911 — the total investment of the Steel Corporation in tangible property, the net earnings, and the ratio of the net earnings to the investment.

The table shows that the net earnings of the Steel Corporation ranged from $62,000,000 in 1904 (its worst year) to $155,000,000 in 1907 (its best year); and averaged $112,000,000 for the ten year period. By the side of such earnings, the profits of the Standard Oil Company, large as they were, seem small indeed. The table shows further that the profits of the Steel Corporation from 1901 to 1910 averaged 12 per cent on its investment. The average rate of profit, however, underestimates the prosperity of the Steel Corporation. In the first place, the investment included a large amount of idle property, particularly undeveloped iron ore lands; and this naturally tended to reduce the rate of profit on the investment. But more important, the profit of 12 per cent covered the entire investment, whether that investment was represented by 5 per cent bonds, 7 per cent preferred stock, or common stock. The rate of profit on the investment represented by common stock was of course much higher than 12 per cent. But just how much higher, it is not possible to say; the Bureau found it impossible to make a satisfactory computation.

NET EARNINGS*

Year ending December 31	Total investment in tangible property. 000 omitted	Amount. 000 omitted	Per cent
1901	$ 698,869	$ 77,741†	14.8‡
1902	763,574	121,502	15.9
1903	806,615	94,156	11.7
1904	818,238	62,491	7.6
1905	874,840	112,830	12.9
1906	947,397	143,393	15.1
1907	1,078,763	155,416	14.4
1908	1,090,425	84,793	7.8
1909	1,146,875	120,807	10.5
1910	1,186,982	127,216	10.7
Average	941,258	112,856	12.0

* The net earnings are not those given in the annual reports of the Steel Corporation; the Bureau has revised the Corporation's figures somewhat. Thus, the Corporation deducted interest on its bonds in determining its net earnings; the Bureau restored these interest payments to the net earnings, as it was desirous of finding out what the property actually earned rather than the distribution of earnings among the different classes of security holders. Other changes were made by the Bureau in arriving at its figures of net earnings.
† Nine months, April to December.
‡ Indicated rate per annum, based on actual earnings for nine months.

The net earnings of the Corporation, the sum available for dividends on its common stock, and the percentage earned and paid on its common stock during the years 1901 to 1911 (the year in which the government suit was brought) are shown in the following table.

In view of the fact that all of the common stock was "water" this record must have been quite gratifying to the stockholders of the Corporation. How much more so must this have been true in 1916, when because of the unusual demands for steel arising out of the war there was earned on the common stock $246,000,000, or 48.46 per cent!

Yet in spite of the large sums expended in the construction of new plants, in spite of the acquisition of important competitors, and in spite of its enormous earnings, the Steel Corporation was not

EARNINGS AND DIVIDENDS OF THE STEEL CORPORATION, 1901 TO 1911

	Net earnings.* 000,000 omitted	Earned on common stock. 000,000 omitted	Earned on common stock Per cent	Paid on common stock Per cent
1901	$ 84†	$34	9.08	2.00
1902	133	54	10.74	4.00
1903	109	25	4.92	3.50
1904	73	5	0.99	. . .
1905	119	43	8.53	. . .
1906	156	72	14.34	1.50
1907	160	79	15.61	2.00
1908	91	20	4.05	2.00
1909	131	53	10.59	2.75
1910	141	62	12.23	5.50
1911	104	30	5.92	5.00

* After deduction of expenses for ordinary repairs and maintenance, interest on bonds, fixed charges of subsidiary companies, and employees' bonus funds.
† Nine months only.

able to maintain the prominent position which it held at its organization in 1901. This is indicated by the table [on the following page], showing the proportion of the country's business done by the Steel Corporation in the various lines during the years 1901 to 1910 (the last year prior to the dissolution suit).

With respect to iron ore, the Steel Corporation maintained fairly well down to 1910 the position which it attained in 1901. Regularly after its formation it produced about 45 per cent of the total output of iron ore (1904 was an off year). In 1908 and 1909, indeed, it produced even more proportionately than in 1901, yet this was because of the purchase in 1907 of the Tennessee Coal, Iron and Railroad Company, producing about 3 per cent of the total output of iron ore. But since 80 to 90 per cent of the ore used for steel making purposes comes from the Lake Superior region, the Steel Corporation's proportion of the Lake shipments gives a better idea of its importance as an ore producer. And these figures tell a somewhat different story.

In 1901 the Steel Corporation controlled over 61 per cent of the ore shipped from the Lake Superior region; in 1910 only 51 per cent. This points to a relative increase in the business done by the independent element.

In the production of coke likewise the Steel Corporation lost ground after its formation. In 1902 — the data are not available for 1901 — it produced 37.4 per cent of the country's output of coke; in

was well situated with respect to its supplies of coking coal.

The percentage of the pig iron production of the country controlled by the Steel Corporation remained practically unchanged between 1901 and 1910. In the former year it produced 42.4 per cent of the total; in the latter 43.0 per cent. Here again the figures are for the total production, rather than the production for steel making purposes; and therefore

PROPORTION OF COUNTRY'S OUTPUT OF IRON ORE, COKE, AND VARIOUS IRON AND STEEL PRODUCTS CONTROLLED BY THE UNITED STATES STEEL CORPORATION, 1901–1910

From annual statistical reports of the American Iron and Steel Association

	'01	'02	'03	'04	'05	'06	'07	'08	'09	'10
IRON ORE:										
Total production	43.9	45.1	43.8	37.9	43.4	43.2	43.3	46.3	45.7	44.3
Shipments from Lake region	61.6	60.4	58.8	53.8	56.0	54.2	54.7	56.0	51.4	51.0
COKE	*	37.4	34.2	36.6	37.9	36.5	30.3	31.3	34.6	32.7
PIG IRON	42.4	44.3	39.9	44.3	43.8	44.2	41.7	43.2	44.8	43.0
PIG IRON, spiegeleisen, ferromanganese	42.9	44.7	40.4	44.6	44.2	44.5	41.9	43.5	45.0	43.3
INGOTS AND CASTINGS:										
Bessemer	70.2	73.9	72.0	69.0	67.4	65.7	64.7	66.2	62.7	61.6
Open-hearth	59.0	52.4	51.0	50.4	51.4	49.6	47.9	48.2	51.8	50.8
TOTAL	66.3	65.7	63.5	61.0	60.2	58.1	56.4	56.1	56.0	54.7
ROLLED PRODUCTS:										
Bessemer steel rails	59.9	65.4	65.6	57.2	53.6	52.6	51.6	58.6	57.3	60.2
Open-hearth steel rails	†	†	†	†	†	†	†	46.3	57.5	57.4
Structural shapes	62.2	57.9	60.3	55.1	54.6	54.6	54.9	47.1	47.1	51.3
Plates and sheets	64.6	59.4	59.9	58.0	57.4	56.3	55.8	51.9	49.8	48.0
Wire rods	77.6	71.5	73.1	71.3	69.9	71.7	71.5	67.9	69.7	67.3
Bars, skelp, etc.	27.3	31.1	29.8	28.6	31.0	33.8	33.9	31.9	39.4	37.6
TOTAL FINISHED ROLLED PRODUCTS	50.1	50.8	51.2	47.8	47.3	48.1	47.5	47.1	48.9	48.1
SECONDARY PRODUCTS:‡										
Wire nails	65.8	64.8	70.6	67.0	66.1	65.5	66.4	61.2	60.7	55.4
Tin plates and Terne plates	*	*	*	*	*	*	*	72.0	61.9	61.0

* Data not available.

† None produced by the Steel Corporation.

‡ These are the only secondary products for which data are available.

1910 only 32.7 per cent. These statistics, however, are for the total output of coke, and not simply for the coke used in the production of iron and steel. The Corporation produced a larger percentage of the coke used in the iron and steel industry than these figures indicate. Controlling, as it did, the choicest coking coal lands in the Connellsville region, it

they do not show the real importance of the Steel Corporation in this field. Yet it is evident that the business of the independents increased considerably, since in 1910 they produced about the same percentage as in 1901, despite the acquisition by the Corporation of the Union Steel Company and the Tennessee Coal, Iron and Railroad Company.

Summarizing for the raw materials, it appears that the Steel Corporation held its own fairly well, though its favorable showing resulted in part from the purchase of important competitors.

The best single index as to the Steel Corporation's position in the steel manufacturing industry is the output of ingots and castings. In 1901 the Corporation produced 66.3 per cent of the country's output of these products, but in each succeeding year it lost ground relatively until by 1910 it produced only 54.7 per cent. And this decline came in spite of the purchase of important competitors. To be sure, the Corporation's total output of ingots and castings has increased enormously since 1901. In 1901 it produced only 8,854,820 tons; in 1910, 14,-179,369 tons. That the company, despite this growth, did not hold its own is due, of course, to the even more rapid growth of its competitors. While the trust did 60 per cent more business in ingots and castings in 1910 than in 1901, its competitors did 154 per cent more. This, moreover, can not be explained by saying that a large concern finds it more difficult to increase its business at the same rate as its smaller competitors, for the competitors of the Steel Corporation not only grew at a faster rate, but in the aggregate showed an absolute increase in business greater than that secured by the Steel Corporation, including, as the latter does, the Carnegie Company, easily the most efficient of the steel companies prior to its incorporation in the trust.[9] Though the Steel Corporation was not able to increase its output as rapidly as its competitors, nevertheless it produced vastly more than its nearest competitor in point of size. In 1911 the

[9] The Steel Corporation's output of ingots and castings increased between 1901 and 1910 by 5,300,000 tons; that of its competitors by 7,200,000 tons.

steel ingot production of the Corporation was 16,856,914 gross tons (55.6 per cent of the country's output), while the largest independent concern — Jones and Laughlin — produced only 1,690,845 tons, or 5.5 per cent.

With respect to the rolled products, taking them as a whole, the Steel Corporation substantially maintained its position. In 1901 it produced 50.1 per cent of the total output of rolled products; in 1910, 48.1 per cent. In individual lines, however, the Steel Corporation lost heavily. In 1901 it produced 62.2 per cent of the structural shapes; in 1910, only 51.3 per cent (the Steel Corporation's output of structural shapes between 1901 and 1910 increased 85 per cent; that of its competitors 188 per cent). In 1901 the Steel Corporation made 64.6 per cent of the plates and sheets; in 1910, only 48.0 per cent (the Steel Corporation increased its output 66 per cent between 1901 and 1910; the independents increased their output 223 per cent). In 1901 the Steel Corporation turned out 77.6 per cent of the wire rods; in 1910, only 67.3 per cent (for the Steel Corporation this represented an increase of 42 per cent; for its competitors, an increase of 139 per cent). In 1901 the Steel Corporation's output of wire nails was 65.8 per cent of the total; in 1910, only 55.4 per cent (between 1901 and 1910 the Corporation's output increased but 9 per cent; that of its competitors 69 per cent).

The maintenance by the Corporation of its position in rolled products as a whole, despite the decrease in these individual lines, seems to have resulted from an increase in the production of bars, skelp, etc., and from the production in 1908 to 1910 of a large proportion of the open-hearth rails, the Corporation having produced none at all prior to 1908. With respect to Bessemer rails, the Corporation produced 59.9 per cent of the country's output in 1901, and though there were ups and downs in the years that followed, it produced in 1910 almost exactly the same percentage. In the maintenance of this position the Corporation was greatly aided by its railroad affiliations. In 1911, for example, one or more directors of the Corporation was to be found on the directorate of sixty-two American railroads, possessing a mileage equal to almost half that of the whole country. It would be strange, indeed, if these connections did not bring the Steel Corporation some business which otherwise would have gone to the independent rail manufacturers.

It is evident that the high degree of control which the Steel Corporation had at the time of its organization was being gradually lost. Even in the lines in which it had a quasi-monopolistic position in 1910, it had lost heavily, almost without exception. This decline had taken place, moreover, in spite of the diversity of the businesses into which the influence of the Steel Corporation ramified. From its organization the officers or directors of the company were at various times on the directorate of a vast number of industrial companies. The Steel Corporation's connections with industrial companies and railroads, all large buyers of iron and steel, naturally attracted to it a great deal of business. Furthermore, the Corporation had powerful moneyed connections. At some time after its organization it had directors on as many as eighty-five different banks and trust companies, and twenty-five insurance companies. In addition, according to Mr. Gary, it made a practice of keeping about seventy-five million dollars in cash on deposit in banks.[10] The government

in its petition went so far as to charge that the Corporation had built up "a system of interlacing of directorates which embraced almost the entire commercial and financial powers of the country."

While the fact of the decline in the relative importance of the Steel Corporation is clear, the explanation thereof is not so clear. Possibly those in charge of the Corporation, fearing dissolution proceedings, did not attempt to retain their original degree of control of the steel business of the country. The decision of the Circuit Court refusing to enter a dissolution decree because the Steel Corporation had not been able to hold its own would appear to justify such a policy. On the other hand, not until after 1910 were any of the great trusts dissolved, and it is therefore doubtful whether fear of the law provides the real explanation. Possibly, to give another explanation, the guiding spirits of the Steel Corporation preferred to maintain the prices of iron and steel products, — even at the loss of a proportionate share in the country's growing business, — as a means of squeezing out the water from the company's stock, and of putting it on a more secure foundation. In support of this view it may be said that during periods of industrial depression the proportion of the Corporation's output to the total was generally smaller than its proportion of capacity, owing to its policy of maintaining prices. Thirdly, perhaps the true explanation is the absence of any important economies in the trust form of organization; the sceptic would seem to find here ground for his scepticism.[11]

Even in the absence of important economies, however, a trust might hold its own, could it avail itself of certain props

[10] On December 31, 1913, none of the competitors of the Corporation had a capitalization equal to the amount of cash held by the Steel Corporation.

[11] There is much testimony as to the ability of the Steel Corporation to eliminate its competitors. Most of the witnesses in the government

to maintain its position. The Standard Oil Company, as we have seen, found its main strength in certain objectionable features, such as rebates, control of pipelines, and unfair selling methods. Had the officials of the Steel Corporation been so minded, or did the nature of the business permit, the Steel Corporation might have followed a similar policy. But such has not been the case. In the first place, the Steel Corporation was not the recipient of rebates from the railroads. Mr. James R. Garfield testified in the steel dissolution case that he made an investigation of the relations of the railways to the Steel Corporation similar to the investigation made into the oil business, and he found no evidence of the Steel Corporation having received any rebates. Judge Woolley, of the District Court, stated that there was nothing in the evidence that suggested that the Steel Corporation used its power as a means of securing rebates; on the contrary it appeared that early in its history the Corporation promulgated a rule against soliciting and accepting rebates. The contrast in this respect with the Standard

suit agreed that the cost of converting the raw materials into the finished products (conversion cost) was practically the same for the Steel Corporation as for the leading independent concerns. Mr. Donner, president of the Cambria Steel Company, and formerly a director of the American Tin Plate Company, testified that in his opinion the Steel Corporation could not put its competitors out of business "without committing suicide," that if the Corporation were to make prices so low that there was no profit for the Cambria concern, there would be nothing left for the Corporation. (Brief for the United States, no. 481, vol. II, Summary of Evidence, p. 855.) A mill with a capacity of 40,000 to 50,000 tons of ingots per month, if properly designed and operated, ought, he said, to compete with the Corporation in any of its plants. (Ibid., p. 868.) Mr. Schwab, president of the Bethlehem Steel Company and formerly president of the Corporation itself, testified that the mill cost of the Corporation at Pittsburg or Gary did not differ materially from the mill cost at Bethlehem; that the limit of metallurgical and mechanical possibilities had been reached, and that the conversion cost in all mills throughout the United States was practically uniform. (Ibid., p. 868.) Mr. Corey, formerly president of the Corporation, declared that the cost of production at the Carnegie works was never materially less after the formation of the Corporation than it had been in 1901, at the time the Carnegie works were acquired. (Ibid., p. 869.) Mr. Farrell, then president of the Corporation, enumerated fourteen different steel companies which the Corporation could not put out of business without committing financial suicide. (Ibid., p. 859.) (Whatever may be the verdict with respect to the leading independent concerns, it is much to be doubted, Mr. Farrell to the contrary notwithstanding, whether some of these fourteen companies, such as the Wheeling Steel and Iron Company — with a steel ingot output of less than 1 per cent of that of the Corporation — produced on large enough scale to compete effectively with the Corporation.) On the other hand, Mr. Campbell, president of the Youngstown Sheet and Tube Company, when asked whether, taking into account the extent of the ore holdings of the Corporation, its ownership of railroads, the extent of its capitalization, the character of men interested in it and their relations to banking circles and railroads, the Corporation had the power to put its competitors out of business, replied, "I think they would have the power; yes, sir . . . I think if Judge Gary would happen to die to-night that there would be a good many steel people that would lie awake until his successor was appointed." (Ibid., pp. 850–851.) Mr. Schwab testified that it cost his company more to make steel rails than it did the Corporation, because his company did not transport its own ore. (Ibid., p. 868.) Judge Gary, the real head of the Steel Corporation, testified in 1908 that the Corporation could produce pig iron cheaper than its competitors; that although the mill costs of production were about the same for the Corporation as for some of the other companies, yet by reason of the control of the best ores the Corporation could undersell them. (Ibid., p. 868.) The conclusion would seem to be that the Corporation by virtue of its ownership of the cream of the ore and coking coal lands and of the iron ore railroads (not to mention its financial connections) had an advantage over its competitors, but that this advantage did not demonstrate the superior economy of the trust form of organization. Rather it demonstrated the many-sidedness of the trust problem and the inability to achieve results in the way of restoring competition except by the adoption of a legislative policy that takes into account the many favoring factors that lie at the basis of the apparent success achieved by some trusts.

Oil Company is noteworthy. The Steel Corporation, with its iron ore railroads, has not, it is true, lived up to its obligations as a common carrier, but the iron ore railroads cut by no means the same figure in this industry as do the crude oil pipe-lines in the oil industry. Moreover, the Steel Corporation did not endeavor to coerce dealers or consumers into dealing with it exclusively. Neither did it resort to local price cutting as a means of restraining competitive business. Whether it would have done so had circumstances permitted can not be said; the conditions, as a matter of fact, did not permit. On this point the Circuit Court said: "Under conditions incident to the steel trade the power of a large company to carry on a ruinous trade war against any particular competitor does not exist in the iron and steel industry. The customers of the great steel companies are large jobbers and the purchasing agents of other companies, who are in the closest touch with every fluctuation of the steel market. The result is that any effort on the part of any one of these great steel companies to inaugurate a trade war by ruinously underselling a competitor would at once, owing to the sensitiveness and interrelated character of the steel market, result in forcing the company that was thus ruinously selling in any particular market or locality to in the same way ruinously lower its prices in every other community." The Steel Corporation therefore could not wage a localized warfare against its competitors. It could, of course, have reduced the prices of articles made by certain competitors without reducing the prices of the articles not made by these competitors, and in this way have subjected these particular competitors to cutthroat competition. But this policy was not followed. It could also have cut prices to

the bone everywhere, yet according to the president of the Cambria Steel Company this would have amounted to an act of suicide. The testimony is ample that the competition of the Steel Corporation, though vigorous, was fair, and conspicuously free from the brutality of which some other trusts have been found guilty. The tariff, it is true, played its part. The iron and steel industry has been a notable recipient of tariff favors, and the combinations and trusts in this industry (notably the tin plate trust) have profited thereby. In fact, some of the trusts of the late nineties would perhaps never have been formed had it not been for the tariff wall, well-nigh insurmountable to foreign competitors. But certainly the tariff was not the mother of the steel trust of 1901; by that time the duty had become nominal. After the removal of the duties from iron and steel products by the Simmons-Underwood bill of 1913, the Steel Corporation for the most part stood on its own feet, unsupported by legislative props,[12] save, of course, such artificial support as was involved in the failure of the government to prevent the Corporation from acquiring a semi-monopoly of the best iron ore deposits, and from utilizing its iron ore railroads to the detriment of its competitors, — subjects to which we now turn.

In view of the fact that the Steel Corporation was losing its hold on the industry, one might have concluded that the wise public policy would have been that of "watchful waiting," that the steel trust in time would disintegrate by virtue of its very unwieldiness. This may prove to be the outcome, yet it must be remembered that the Steel Corporation is un-

[12] Not all iron and steel products were placed on the free list. Thus, the duty on tubes and pipes was made 20 per cent ad valorem; on tin plate 15 per cent; and on structural shapes 10 per cent.

usually well intrenched in the matter of the essential natural resources. The important elements which go into the manufacture of pig iron (the foundation of the steel manufacture) are iron ore, coking coal, and limestone. Of these the iron ore is the most important, and the Steel Corporation, in 1911, when the Report of the Commissioner of Corporations was published, held approximately 75 per cent of all the commercially available iron ore of the Lake Superior district, the ore of this district being the basis of the iron and steel industry of the country. (About 85 per cent of the country's output of iron ore came at that time from the Lake Superior district.) In addition, the Steel Corporation owned immense deposits of iron ore in the South and in other sections, even including deposits in Cuba. Mr. Gary, the chairman of the Steel Corporation, admitted in his testimony before the House Ways and Means Committee in 1908 that the Corporation practically controlled the ultimate ore supply of the country.

The testimony of Mr. Schwab before the Stanley Committee is also significant. Mr. Schwab gave it as his opinion that there would not be any great development in the iron and steel business by new enterprises, because of the difficulty of securing a sufficiently large supply of raw material. Only a concern possessing a large reserve of ore could afford to make the large investment required to produce iron and steel economically, and the greater part of the ore on this continent was already owned or leased by existing companies.

The dominating position of the Steel Corporation in the ore industry was heightened through its ownership of iron ore railroads. The Steel Corporation owned the Duluth and Iron Range, and the Duluth, Missabe and Northern, the two most important ore roads in the Lake Superior region.[13] The freight rates charged by these roads were very high, their operating expenses were very low (the operating ratio in 1910 was 36.5 per cent for one and below 30 per cent for the other, against an average of 66 per cent for the whole country); and as a result these ore roads were immensely profitable. In 1911 a considerable reduction in the rates on iron ore was made by the carriers, but, according to the Commissioner of Corporations, they were still excessive.[14] These high rates not only contributed greatly to the enormous earnings of the Steel Corporation, but they imposed a burden on such of its competitors as were obliged to ship their ore over these roads, — for none of the competitors of the Corporation owned any railroads carrying iron ore from the ore fields to the Lake ports. This situation would seem to have called for the application of the principle of the commodity clause; the interests of the public would seem to have required that the Steel Corporation divest itself of its iron ore railroads, and thus remove the inducement which they had to restrain the independent operations by means of excessive freight rates and discrimination in service.

After the report of the Bureau of Corporations was published, the Steel Corporation cancelled the lease it held of the valuable ore lands of the Great Northern Railway system. This lease had been made in 1907 in order to prevent any one else making use of these ore lands (the unusually high rate of royalty leads to this conclusion). It was provided that

[13] These two roads handled about two-thirds of the total ore traffic of the Lake Superior district.

[14] A further reduction was ordered in 1915 by the Interstate Commerce Commission.

the lease might be cancelled by the Steel Corporation on January 1, 1915, upon giving two years' notice. On October 17, 1911, the Finance Committee of the Steel Corporation, influenced possibly by the prospect of the filing of a government bill — one was filed on October 26 — decided to cancel the lease on January 1, 1915. This action opened up a large supply of excellent ore, which might be made use of by independent operations.

But of more importance as bearing on the ability of the Steel Corporation to effect a monopoly because of a control of the iron ore is the fact that the high class Lake Superior ores owned by the Steel Corporation have become less and less the basis of the steel industry. New fields were developed, and ores which a few years ago were regarded as unusable can now be worked under the improved methods in vogue. The Bethlehem Steel Company, for example, gets its iron ore from the Adirondack mountains in New York, from Sweden, Chili, and Cuba.[15] This company and other tidewater concerns became entirely independent of Lake Superior ore, and after the passage of the Simmons-Underwood bill were not hampered by a duty on foreign ore. The Colorado Fuel and Iron Company has its ore in Wyoming, New Mexico, and Utah; and is also independent of Lake Superior ore. Present indications, therefore, are that the establishment of a trust based on control of the iron ore will prove futile because of new discoveries and improved methods.[16] And such may in other industries frequently prove to be the case. But certainly this will not be true of all industries, and therefore a definite, far-sighted policy with respect to our natural resources would seem to be but the part of wisdom.

The foregoing considerations, however, relate to the future. Competition in production continues quite active, and the independents are steadily growing in strength and importance. Yet this competition has not made itself felt fully with respect to prices; competition in prices has been materially restrained by various means, — pools, trade meetings, and dinners. At the time of the organization of the Steel Corporation and for several years thereafter a number of the constituent companies of the Corporation allotted trade and fixed prices by means of pooling agreements. In the year 1904 the president of the Corporation ordered the subsidiaries to withdraw from these pools. Nevertheless shortly thereafter representatives of the same concerns that had been parties to the pools held trade meetings, and at these meetings there were reached understandings with respect to prices by means of which the price level was maintained as effectually as under the agreements. The legality of these meetings was questioned, and in 1907 they were abandoned.[17] They were soon followed, however, by the famous Gary dinners, — another device for substituting cooperation for competition as a regulator of prices.

The first of these dinners was held in New York City on November 20, 1907. The panic of October, 1907, had demoralized the steel trade, and the dinner was held to discuss the proper method of handling the situation. There were pres-

15 Moreover, new deposits in the Lake Superior district were discovered, thus reducing the Corporation's percentage of the total.

16 According to the Steel Corporation its ore holdings in the Lake Superior district amount to less than 45.6 per cent of the known and developed ores of the first quality.

17 According to the Brief for the Steel Corporation (no. 481), p. 219, they were abandoned in October, 1906.

ent a number of manufacturers of iron and steel, controlling among them at least 90 per cent of the trade. Mr. Gary, in his testimony in the government suit, explained the reason for holding the dinner. "My purpose was . . . to prevent the demoralization of business, to maintain so far as practicable the stability of business and to prevent, if I could, not by agreement, but by exhortation, the wide and sudden fluctuation of prices which would be injurious to everyone interested in the business of the iron and steel manufacturers."

This "exhortation" to his fellow-manufacturers was supported by an elaborate scheme for controlling prices. As a result of the dinner a general Advisory Committee of five members was appointed, Mr. Gary being chairman. This committee was empowered to appoint sub-committees; and it did appoint nine such committees, one on ore and pig iron, another on rails and billets, and so on. The Steel Corporation was well represented on these committees, having two representatives on the General Committee, and one representative on each of the nine sub-committees. The sub-committees held meetings in various parts of the country with more or less regularity for several months. The president of the Youngstown Sheet and Tube Company was made a member of the sub-committee on sheets and plates. He testified in the government suit that shortly after the dinner of November 20, 1907, he attended a meeting in Pittsburg of the manufacturers of tin plate and sheet steel, at which there were present 90 per cent of the manufacturers of sheet steel; that this meeting was an outgrowth of the first Gary dinner; and that at this meeting each manufacturer was questioned in regard to his percentage of the business, and his mill operations. When

the maintenance of the market prices was discussed, what was in mind was the prices published by the subsidiaries of the Steel Corporation. He further testified that, when he was chairman of a sub-committee meeting, he would ask those present to state whether they thought the price was too high, or whether it was too low, and that, when a consensus of opinion had been reached, he would call on each one to state what policy he would follow with respect to prices. He made it clear to the members that agreements were illegal; and that there would be no agreement, no penalties, and no restriction of output. But in response to inquiry from the government examiner he stated that he thought that there was a general understanding "that their policy would be to market their product at the then prevailing price until they notified their competitors that they wanted to change their price." The witness also attended the meetings of the tube manufacturers and of the manufacturers of billets and sheet bars, and they were conducted on substantially the same basis. The president of the McKeesport Tin Plate Company admitted that the effect of the meetings was to maintain a steady price, and that after prices were announced he would feel under a moral obligation to sell at that price until he notified his competitors of an intention to change. Much additional testimony might be cited; but the following excerpt from the testimony of the president of the Steel Corporation from 1903 to December 31, 1910, will suffice:

Q. State whether or not it was the purpose, in the creation of these sub-committees to reach a general understanding as to prices of iron and steel products and to bring about the maintenance of them.

The Witness. Yes.

Q. Were there understandings as to what those prices would be?

The Witness. There were.

Q. Were the prices maintained or not as a result of those understandings?

The Witness. They were.

It seems clear that through the General Committee and the sub-committees the manufacturers of steel cooperated, not only in maintaining the market price, but also in making the market price identical with that quoted by the subsidiaries of the Steel Corporation.

In February, 1909, this policy of cooperation was temporarily abandoned. Business had so declined in volume that the independents refused to abide by the "understandings," and sold at prices determined by themselves. The Steel Corporation attempted for a time to maintain prices by itself, but soon abandoned the attempt, and established an open market in steel products, except in rails. In October, 1909, the meetings of the steel manufacturers at luncheons and dinners were resumed, and the result was the restoration of the policy of cooperation. In the fall of 1910 and the early part of 1911 there were further meetings of the officials of the Steel Corporation with the other steel manufacturers.

Fortunately the speeches made at the dinner of January 11, 1911, have been preserved, and these clearly show the workings of the Gary dinners. In his speech Mr. Gary said in part:

We have something better to guide and control us in our business methods than a contract which depends upon written or verbal promises with a penalty attached. We, as men, as gentlemen, as friends, as neighbors, having been in close communication and contact during the last few years, have reached a point where we entertain for one another respect and affectionate regard. We have reached a position so high in our lines of activity that we are bound to protect one another; and when a man reaches a position where his honor is at stake, where even more than life itself is concerned, where he can not act or fail to act except with a distinct and clear understanding that his honor is involved, then he has reached a position that is more binding on him than any written or verbal contract.

In his speech Mr. Gary further said that in his opinion it would be a mistake to reduce prices at that time. At this same dinner a representative of Jones and Laughlin said in part, "I hope it will be the consensus of opinion here to-night that we will maintain the present prices." The president of the Ashland Steel Company said that so far as his company was concerned, "we are ready and willing to still cooperate to do what we can to maintain prices." Mr. Gary, during the course of the dinner, called on practically all of the leading steel manufacturers, and each, almost without exception, expressed himself as in favor of maintaining the existing prices, or as ready to support the cooperative movement with respect to prices.

Whether as a result of the investigation of the Stanley Committee of the House of Representatives or in anticipation of the government suit, the Gary dinners came to an end in 1911, and judging from the movement of prices, the cooperative arrangement was given up. With respect to these dinners the Stanley Committee said:

We think the conclusion is irresistible that the Gary dinners were instituted as a means of conveying to the entire iron and steel industry information as to what the attitude of the United States Steel Corporation was upon the questions of output and prices and of impressing upon all engaged in the industry that it was the part of wisdom and prudence to govern themselves accordingly. We further believe that by this means prices were maintained, output restricted, competition stifled, and trade restrained, just as certainly, just as effectively, and just as unlawfully as had been done under the discarded pooling agreements of former years.

Perhaps the best evidence of the success of the policy of cooperation, promoted by pools and dinners, is the course of the price of Bessemer steel rails. From 1867 to 1900 (the year before the formation of the steel trust) the price of steel rails varied every year; in no two years during all this period did it continue the same. Prior to the formation of the Steel Corporation there was severe competition in steel rails, and the price fell from $28 per ton in 1896 to $17 per ton in 1898. A combination then raised the price for a time to $35, but early in 1901 it went as low as $26. In April, 1901, the Steel Corporation began operations; in May the price of rails was fixed at $28 per ton; and the price remained at that figure up to the date of the government suit, having been effectively controlled by the Steel Corporation in cooperation with the independent steel manufacturers. This price of $28, it may be noted, was some $10 per ton higher than the prices that prevailed during 1897–1898, when there was competition between the Carnegie Steel Company and the Illinois Steel Company; though the prices of 1897–1898 yielded these companies a substantial profit. The ability of the Steel Corporation to maintain the price of steel rails at an arbitrary figure, despite marked fluctuations in demand[18] and in manufacturing costs, abundantly testifies to the tremendous power of this mammoth organization.

[18] In 1901, 99.9 per cent of the rails sold were Bessemer rails. Since that date Bessemer rails have been largely superseded by open-hearth rails. In 1912 only one third of the rails sold were Bessemer rails.

Theodore Roosevelt: THE TRUSTS, THE PEOPLE, AND THE SQUARE DEAL

THE suit against the Steel Trust by the Government has brought vividly before our people the need of reducing to order our chaotic Government policy as regards business. As President, in Messages to Congress I repeatedly called the attention of that body and of the public to the inadequacy of the Anti-Trust Law by itself to meet business conditions and secure justice to the people, and to the further fact that it might, if left unsupplemented by additional legislation, work mischief, with no compensating advantage; and I urged as strongly as I knew how that the policy followed with relation to railways in connection with the Inter-State Commerce Law should be followed by the National Government as regards all great business concerns; and therefore that, as a first step, the powers of the Bureau of Corporations should be greatly enlarged, or

Reprinted by permission from *Outlook*, Vol. 99, No. 12 (November 18, 1911), 649–656.

else that there should be created a Governmental board or commission, with powers somewhat similar to those of the Inter-State Commerce Commission, but covering the whole field of inter-State business, exclusive of transportation (which should, by law, be kept wholly separate from ordinary industrial business, all common ownership of the industry and the railway being forbidden). In the end I have always believed that it would also be necessary to give the National Government complete power over the organization and capitalization of all business concerns engaged in inter-State commerce.

A member of my Cabinet with whom even more than with the various Attorneys-General, I went over every detail of this trust situation, was the one time Secretary of the Interior, Mr. James R. Garfield. He writes me as follows concerning the suit against the Steel Corporation:

Nothing appeared before the House Committee that made me believe we were deceived by Judge Gary.

This, I think, is a case that shows clearly the difference between destructive litigation and constructive legislation. I have not yet seen a full copy of the Government's petition, but our papers give nothing that indicates any kind of unfair or dishonest competition such as existed in both the Standard Oil and Tobacco cases. As I understand it, the competitors of the Steel Company have steadily increased in strength during the last six or seven years. Furthermore, the per cent of the business done by the Steel Corporation has decreased during that time. As you will remember, at our first conference with Judge Gary, the Judge stated that it was the desire and purpose of the Company to conform to what the Government wished, it being the purpose of the Company absolutely to obey the law both in spirit and letter. Throughout the time that I had charge of the investiga-

tion, and while we were in Washington, I do not know of a single instance where the Steel Company refused any information requested; but, on the contrary, aided in every possible way our investigation.

The position now taken by the Government is absolutely destructive of legitimate business, because they outline no rule of conduct for business of any magnitude. It is absurd to say that the courts can lay down such rules. The most the courts can do is to find as legal or illegal the particular transactions brought before them. Hence, after years of tedious litigation there would be no clear-cut rule for future action. This method of procedure is dealing with the device, not the result, and drives business to the elaboration of clever devices, each of which must be tested in the courts.

I have yet to find a better method of dealing with the anti-trust situation than that suggested by the bill which we agreed upon in the last days of your Administration. That bill should be used as a basis for legislation, and there could be incorporated upon it whatever may be determined wise regarding the direct control and supervision of the National Government, either through a commission similar to the Inter-State Commerce Commission or otherwise.

Before taking up the matter in its large aspect, I wish to say one word as to one feature of the Government suit against the Steel Corporation. One of the grounds for the suit is the acquisition by the Steel Corporation of the Tennessee Coal and Iron Company; and it has been alleged, on the authority of the Government officials engaged in carrying on the suit, that as regards this transaction I was misled by the representatives of the Steel Corporation, and that the facts were not accurately or truthfully laid before me. This statement is not correct. I believed at the time that the facts in the case were as represented to me on behalf of the Steel Corporation, and my further knowledge has convinced me that this was true. I believed at the time that the representatives of the Steel Corporation told me the truth as to the change that would be worked in the percentage of the business which the proposed acquisition would give the Steel Corporation, and further inquiry has convinced me that they did so. I was not misled. The representatives of the Steel Corporation told me the truth as to what the effect of the action at that time would be, and any statement that I was misled or that the representatives of the Steel Corporation did not thus tell me the truth as to the facts of the case is itself not in accordance with the truth. In The Outlook of August 19 last I gave in full the statement I had made to the Investigating Committee of the House of Representatives on this matter. That statement is accurate, and I reaffirm everything I therein said, not only as to what occurred, but also as to my belief in the wisdom and propriety of my action — indeed, the action not merely was wise and proper, but it would have been a calamity from every standpoint had I failed to take it. On page 137 of the printed report of the testimony before the Committee will be found Judge Gary's account of the meeting between himself and Mr. Frick and Mr. Root and myself. This account states the facts accurately. It has been alleged that the purchase by the Steel Corporation of the property of the Tennessee Coal and Iron Company gave the Steel Corporation practically a monoply of the Southern iron ores — that is, of the iron ores south of the Potomac and the Ohio. My information, which I have every reason to believe is accurate and not successfully to be challenged, is that, of these Southern iron ores the Steel Corporation has, including the property gained from the

Tennessee Coal and Iron Company, less than 20 per cent — perhaps not over 16 per cent. This is a very much smaller percentage than the percentage it holds of the Lake Superior ores, which even after the surrender of the Hill lease will be slightly over 50 per cent. According to my view, therefore, and unless — which I do not believe possible — these figures can be successfully challenged, the acquisition of the Tennessee Coal and Iron Company's ores in no way changed the situation as regards making the Steel Corporation a monopoly.[1] The showing as to the percentage of production of all kinds of steel ingots and steel castings in the United States by the Steel Corporation and by all other manufacturers respectively makes an even stronger case. It makes the case even stronger than I put it in my testimony before the Investigating Committee, for I was scrupulously careful to make statements that erred, if at all, against my own position. It appears from the figures of production that in 1901 the Steel Corporation had to its credit nearly 66 per cent of the total production as against a little over 34 per cent by all other steel manufacturers. The percentage then shrank steadily, until in 1906, the year before the acquisition of the Tennessee Coal and Iron properties, the percentage was a little under 58 per cent. In spite of the acquisition of these properties, the following year, 1907, the total percentage shrank slightly, and this shrinking has continued until in 1910 the total percentage of the Steel Corporation is but a little over 54 per cent, and the percentage by all other steel manufacturers but a frac-

[1] My own belief is that our Nation should long ago have adopted the policy of merely leasing for a term of years mineral-bearing land; but it is the fault of us ourselves, of the people, not of the Steel Corporation, that this policy has not been adopted.

tion less than 46 per cent. Of the 54.3 per cent produced by the Steel Corporation 1.9 per cent is produced by the former Tennessee Coal and Iron Company. In other words, these figures show that the acquisition of the Tennessee Coal and Iron Company did not in the slightest degree change the situation, and that during the ten years which include the acquisition of these properties by the Steel Corporation the percentage of total output of steel manufacturers in this country by the Steel Corporation has shrunk from nearly 66 per cent to but a trifle over 54 per cent. I do not believe that these figures can be successfully controverted, and if not successfully controverted they show clearly not only that the acquisition of the Tennessee Coal and Iron properties wrought no change in the status of the Steel Corporation, but that the Steel Corporation during the decade has steadily lost, instead of gained, in monopolistic character.

So much for the facts in this particular case. Now for the general subject. When my Administration took office, I found, not only that there had been little real enforcement of the Anti-Trust Law and but little more effective enforcement of the Inter-State Commerce Law, but also that the decisions were so chaotic and the laws themselves so vaguely drawn, or at least interpreted in such widely varying fashions, that the biggest business men tended to treat both laws as dead letters. The series of actions by which we succeeded in making the Inter-State Commerce Law an efficient and most useful instrument in regulating the transportation of the country and exacting justice from the big railways without doing them injustice — while, indeed, on the contrary, securing them against injustice — need not here be related. The Anti-Trust Law it was also necessary to

enforce as it had never hitherto been enforced, both because it was on the statute-books and because it was imperative to teach the masters of the biggest corporations in the land that they were not, and would not be permitted to regard themselves as, above the law. Moreover, where the combination has really been guilty of misconduct the law serves a useful purpose, and in such cases as those of the Standard Oil and Tobacco Trusts, if effectively enforced, the law confers a real and great good.

Suits were brought against the most powerful corporations in the land, which we were convinced had clearly and beyond question violated the Anti-Trust Law. These suits were brought with great care, and only where we felt so sure of our facts that we could be fairly certain that there was a likelihood of success. As a matter of fact, in most of the important suits we were successful. It was imperative that these suits should be brought, and very real good was achieved by bringing them, for it was only these suits that made the great masters of corporate capital in America fully realize that they were the servants and not the masters of the people, that they were subject to the law, and that they would not be permitted to be a law unto themselves; and the corporations against which we proceed had sinned, not merely by being big (which we did not regard as in itself a sin), but by being guilty of unfair practices towards their competitors, and by procuring unfair advantages from the railways. But the resulting situation has made it evident that the Anti-Trust Law is not adequate to meet the situation that has grown up because of modern business conditions and the accompanying tremendous increase in the business use of vast quantities of corporate wealth. As I have said, this was already evident to my mind when I was President, and in communications to Congress I repeatedly stated the facts. But when I made these communications there were still plenty of people who did not believe that we would succeed in the suits that had been instituted against the Standard Oil, the Tobacco, and other corporations, and it was impossible to get the public as a whole to realize what the situation was. Sincere zealots who believed that all combinations could be destroyed and the old-time conditions of unregulated competition restored, insincere politicians who knew better but made believe that they thought whatever their constituents wished them to think, crafty reactionaries who wished to see on the statute-books laws which they believed unenforceable, and the almost solid "Wall Street crowd" or representatives of "big business" who at that time opposed with equal violence both wise and necessary and unwise and improper regulation of business — all fought against the adoption of a sane, effective, and far-reaching policy.

It is a vitally necessary thing to have the persons in control of big trusts of the character of the Standard Oil Trust and Tobacco Trust taught that they are under the law, just as it was a necessary thing to have the Sugar Trust taught the same lesson in drastic fashion by Mr. Henry L. Stimson when he was United States District Attorney in the city of New York. But to attempt to meet the whole problem not by administrative governmental action but by a succession of law-suits is hopeless from the standpoint of working out a permanently satisfactory solution. Moreover, the results sought to be achieved are achieved only in extremely insufficient and fragmentary measure by breaking up all big corporations, whether they have behaved well or

ill, into a number of little corporations which it is perfectly certain will be largely, and perhaps altogether, under the same control. Such action is harsh and mischievous if the corporation is guilty of nothing except its size; and where, as in the case of the Standard Oil, and especially the Tobacco, trusts, the corporation has been guilty of immoral and anti-social practices, there is need for far more drastic and thoroughgoing action than any that has been taken, under the recent decree of the Supreme Court. In the case of the Tobacco Trust, for instance, the settlement in the Circuit Court, in which the representatives of the Government seem inclined to concur, practically leaves all of the companies still substantially under the control of the twenty-nine original defendants. Such a result is lamentable from the standpoint of justice. The decision of the Circuit Court, if allowed to stand, means that the Tobacco Trust has merely been obliged to change its clothes, that none of the real offenders have received any real punishment, while, as the New York "Times," a pro-trust paper, says, the tobacco concerns, in their new clothes, are in positions of "ease and luxury," and "immune from prosecution under the law."

Surely, miscarriage of justice is not too strong a term to apply to such a result when considered in connection with what the Supreme Court said of this Trust. That great Court in its decision used language which in spite of its habitual and severe self-restraint in stigmatizing wrong-doing, yet unhesitatingly condemns the Tobacco Trust for moral turpitude, saying that the case shows an "ever-present manifestation . . . of conscious wrongdoing" by the Trust, whose history is "replete with the doing of acts which it was the obvious purpose of the statute to forbid . . . demonstrative of the existence from the beginning of a purpose to acquire dominion and control of the tobacco trade, not by the mere exertion of the ordinary right to contract and to trade, but by methods devised in order to monopolize the trade by driving competitors out of business, which were ruthlessly carried out upon the assumption that to work upon the fears or play upon the cupidity of competitors would make success possible." The letters from and to various officials of the Trust, which were put in evidence, show a literally astounding and horrifying indulgence by the Trust in wicked and depraved business methods — such as the "endeavor to cause a strike in their [a rival business firm's] factory," or the "shutting off the market" of an independent tobacco firm by "taking the necessary steps to give them a warm reception," or forcing importers into a price agreement by causing and continuing "a demoralization of the business for such length of time as may be deemed desirable" (I quote from the letters). A Trust guilty of such conduct should be absolutely disbanded, and the only way to prevent the repetition of such conduct is by strict Government supervision, and not merely by lawsuits.

The Anti-Trust Law cannot meet the whole situation, nor can any modification of the principle of the Anti-Trust Law avail to meet the whole situation. The fact is that many of the men who have called themselves Progressives, and who certainly believe that they are Progressives, represent in reality in this matter not progress at all but a kind of sincere rural toryism. These men believe that it is possible by strengthening the Anti-Trust Law to restore business to the competitive conditions of the middle of the last century. Any such effort is fore-

doomed to end in failure, and, if successful, would be mischievous to the last degree. Business cannot be successfully conducted in accordance with the practices and theories of sixty years ago unless we abolish steam, electricity, big cities, and, in short, not only all modern business and modern industrial conditions, but all the modern conditions of our civilization. The effort to restore competition as it was sixty years ago, and to trust for justice solely to this proposed restoration of competition, is just as foolish as if we should go back to the flintlocks of Washington's Continentals as a substitute for modern weapons of precision. The effort to prohibit all combinations, good or bad, is bound to fail, and ought to fail; when made, it merely means that some of the worst combinations are not checked and that honest business is checked. Our purpose should be, not to strangle business as an incident of strangling combinations, but to regulate big corporations in thoroughgoing and effective fashion, so as to help legitimate business as an incident to thoroughly and completely safeguarding the interests of the people as a whole. Against all such increase of Government regulation the argument is raised that it would amount to a form of Socialism. This argument is familiar; it is precisely the same as that which was raised against the creation of the Inter-State Commerce Commission, and of all the different utilities commissions in the different States, as I myself saw, thirty years ago, when I was a legislator at Albany, and these questions came up in connection with our State Government. Nor can action be effectively taken by any one State. Congress alone has power under the Constitution effectively and thoroughly and at all points to deal with inter-State commerce, and where Congress, as it should do, provides laws that will give the Nation full jurisdiction over the whole field, then that jurisdiction becomes, of necessity, exclusive — although until Congress does act affirmatively and thoroughly it is idle to expect that the States will or ought to rest content with non-action on the part of both Federal and State authorities. This statement, by the way, applies also to the question of "usurpation" by any one branch of our Government of the rights of another branch. It is contended that in these recent decisions the Supreme Court legislated; so it did; and it had to; because Congress had signally failed to do *its* duty by legislating. For the Supreme Court to nullify an act of the Legislature as unconstitutional except on the clearest grounds is usurpation; to interpret such an act in an obviously wrong sense is usurpation; but where the legislative body persistently leaves open a field which it is absolutely imperative, from the public standpoint, to fill, then no possible blame attaches to the official or officials who step in because they have to, and who then do the needed work in the interest of the people. The blame in such cases lies with the body which has been derelict, and not with the body which reluctantly makes good the dereliction.

A quarter of a century ago, Senator Cushman K. Davis, a statesman who amply deserved the title of statesman, a man of the highest courage, of the sternest adherence to the principles laid down by an exacting sense of duty, an unflinching believer in democracy, who was as little to be cowed by a mob as by a plutocrat, and moreover a man who possessed the priceless gift of imagination, a gift as important to a statesman as to a historian, in an address delivered at the annual commencement of the University of Michigan on July 1, 1886, spoke as follows of corporations:

Feudalism, with its domains, its untaxed lords, their retainers, its exemptions and privileges, made war upon the aspiring spirit of humanity, and fell with all its grandeurs. Its spirit walks the earth and haunts the institutions of to-day, in the great corporations, with the control of the National highways, their occupation of great domains, their power to tax, their cynical contempt for the law, their sorcery to debase most gifted men to the capacity of splendid slaves, their pollution of the ermine of the judge and the robe of the Senator, their aggregation in one man of wealth so enormous as to make Croesus seem a pauper, their picked, paid, and skilled retainers who are summoned by the message of electricity and appear upon the wings of steam. If we look into the origin of feudalism and of the modern corporations — those Dromios of history — we find that the former originated in a strict paternalism, which is scouted by modern economists, and that the latter has grown from an unrestrained freedom of action, aggression, and development, which they commend as the very ideal of political wisdom. *Laissez-faire,* says the professor, when it often means bind and gag that the strongest may work his will. It is a plea for the survival of the fittest — for the strongest male to take possession of the herd by a process of extermination. If we examine this battle cry of political polemics, we find that it is based upon the conception of the divine right of property, and the preoccupation by older or more favored or more alert or richer men or nations, of territory, of the forces of nature, of machinery, of all the functions of what we call civilization. Some of these men, who are really great, follow these conceptions to their conclusions with dauntless intrepidity.

When Senator Davis spoke, few men of great power had the sympathy and the vision necessary to perceive the menace contained in the growth of corporations;

and the men who did see the evil were struggling blindly to get rid of it, not by frankly meeting the new situation with new methods, but by insisting upon the entirely futile effort to abolish what modern conditions had rendered absolutely inevitable. Senator Davis was under no such illusion. He realized keenly that it was absolutely impossible to go back to an outworn social status, and that we must abandon definitely the *laissez-faire* theory of political economy, and fearlessly champion a system of increased Governmental control, paying no heed to the cries of the worthy people who denounce this as Socialistic. He saw that, in order to meet the inevitable increase in the power of corporations produced by modern industrial conditions, it would be necessary to increase in like fashion the activity of the sovereign power which alone could control such corporations. As has been aptly said; the only way to meet a billion-dollar corporation is by invoking the protection of a hundred-billion-dollar government; in other words, of the National Government, for no State Government is strong enough both to do justice to corporations and to exact justice from them. Said Senator Davis in this admirable address, which should be reprinted and distributed broadcast:

The liberty of the individual has been annihilated by the logical process constructed to maintain it. We have come to a political deification of Mammon. *Laissez-faire* is not utterly blameworthy. It begat modern democracy, and made the modern republic possible. There can be no doubt of that. But there it began its limit of political benefaction, and began to incline toward the point where extremes meet. . . . To every assertion that the people in their collective capacity of a government ought to exert their indefeasible right to self-defense, it is said you touch the sacred rights of property.

The Senator then goes on to say that we now have to deal with an oligarchy of wealth, and that the Government must develop power sufficient enough to enable it to do the task.

Few will dispute the fact that the present situation is not satisfactory, and cannot be put on a permanently satisfactory basis unless we put an end to the period of groping and declare for a fixed policy, a policy which shall clearly define and punish wrong-doing, which shall put a stop to the iniquities done in the name of business, but which shall do strict equity to business. We demand that big business give the people a square deal; in return we must insist that when any one engaged in big business honestly endeavors to do right he shall himself be given a square deal; and the first, and most elementary, kind of square deal is to give him in advance full information as to just what he can, and what he cannot, legally and properly do. It is absurd, and much worse than absurd, to treat the deliberate lawbreaker as on an exact par with the man eager to obey the law, whose only desire is to find out from some competent Governmental authority what the law is, and then to live up to it. Moreover, it is absurd to treat the size of a corporation as in itself a crime. As Judge Hook says in his opinion in the Standard Oil Case; "Magnitude of business does not alone constitute a monopoly . . . the genius and industry of man when kept to ethical standards still have full play, and what he achieves is his . . . success and magnitude of business, the rewards of fair and honorable endeavor [are not forbidden] . . . [the public welfare is threatened only when success is attained] by wrongful or unlawful methods." Size may, and in my opinion does, make a corporation fraught with potential menace to the community; and may, and in my opinion should, therefore make it incumbent upon the community to exercise through its administrative (not merely through its judicial) officers a strict supervision over that corporation in order to see that it does not go wrong; but the size in itself does not signify wrong-doing, and should not be held to signify wrong-doing.

Not only should any huge corporation which has attained its position by unfair methods, and by interference with the rights of others, by demoralizing and corrupt practices, in short, by sheer baseness and wrong-doing, be broken up, but it should be made the business of some administrative governmental body, by constant supervision, to see that it does not come together again, save under such strict control as shall insure the community against all repetition of the bad conduct — and it should never be permitted thus to assemble its parts as long as these parts are under the control of the original offenders, for actual experience has shown that these men are, from the standpoint of the people at large, unfit to be trusted with the power implied in the management of a large corporation. But nothing of importance is gained by breaking up a huge inter-State and international industrial organization *which has not offended otherwise than by its size*, into a number of small concerns without any attempt to regulate the way in which those concerns as a whole shall do business. Nothing is gained by depriving the American Nation of good weapons wherewith to fight in the great field of international industrial competition. Those who would seek to restore the days of unlimited and uncontrolled competition, and who believe that a panacea for our industrial and economic ills is to be found in the mere breaking up of all big corporations, simply because

they are big, are attempting not only the impossible, but what, if possible, would be undesirable. They are acting as we should act if we tried to dam the Mississippi, to stop its flow outright. The effort would be certain to result in failure and disaster; we would have attempted the impossible, and so would have achieved nothing, or worse than nothing. But by building levees along the Mississippi, not seeking to dam the stream, but to control it, we are able to achieve our object and to confer inestimable good in the course of so doing.

This Nation should definitely adopt the policy of attacking, not the mere fact of combination, but the evils and wrongdoing which so frequently accompany combination. The fact that a combination is very big is ample reason for exercising a close and jealous supervision over it, because its size renders it potent for mischief; but it should not be punished unless it actually does the mischief; it should merely be so supervised and controlled as to guarantee us, the people, against its doing mischief. We should not strive for a policy of unregulated competition and of the destruction of all big corporations, that is, of all the most efficient business industries in the land. Nor should we persevere in the hopeless experiment of trying to regulate these industries by means only of lawsuits, each lasting several years, and of uncertain results. We should enter upon a course of supervision, control, and regulation of these great corporations — a regulation which we should not fear, if necessary, to bring to the point of control of monopoly prices, just as in exceptional cases railway rates are now regulated. Either the Bureau of Corporations should be authorized, or some other governmental body similar to the Inter-State Commerce Commission should be created, to exercise this supervision, this authoritative control. When once immoral business practices have been eliminated by such control, competition will thereby be again revived as a healthy factor, although not as formerly an all-sufficient factor, in keeping the general business situation sound. Wherever immoral business practices still obtain — as they obtained in the cases of the Standard Oil Trust and Tobacco Trust — the Anti-Trust Law can be invoked; and wherever such a prosecution is successful, and the courts declare a corporation to possess a monopolistic character, then that corporation should be completely dissolved, and the parts ought never to be again assembled save on whatever terms and under whatever conditions may be imposed by the governmental body in which is vested the regulatory power. Methods can readily be devised by which corporations sincerely desiring to act fairly and honestly can on their own initiative come under this thoroughgoing administrative control by the Government and thereby be free from the working of the Anti-Trust Law. But the law will remain to be invoked against wrong-doers; and under such conditions it could be invoked far more vigorously and successfully than at present.

It is not necessary in an article like this to attempt to work out such a plan in detail. It can assuredly be worked out. Moreover, in my opinion, substantially some such plan must be worked out or business chaos will continue. Wrongdoing such as was perpetrated by the Standard Oil Trust, and especially by the Tobacco Trust, should not only be punished, but if possible punished in the persons of the chief authors and beneficiaries of the wrong, far more severely than at present. But punishment should not be the only, or indeed the main, end

in view. Our aim should be a policy of construction and not one of destruction. Our aim should not be to punish the men who have made a big corporation successful merely because they have made it big and successful, but to exercise such thoroughgoing supervision and control over them as to insure their business skill being exercised in the interest of the public and not against the public interest. Ultimately, I believe that this control should undoubtedly indirectly or directly extend to dealing with all questions connected with their treatment of their employees, including the wages, the hours of labor, and the like. Not only is the proper treatment of a corporation, from the standpoint of the managers, shareholders, and employees, compatible with securing from that corporation the best standard of public service, but when the effort is wisely made it results in benefit both to the corporation and to the public. The success of Wisconsin in dealing with the corporations within her borders, so as both to do them justice and to exact justice in return from them toward the public, has been signal; and this Nation should adopt a progressive policy in substance akin to the progressive policy not merely formulated in theory but reduced to actual practice with such striking success in Wisconsin.

To sum up, then. It is practically impossible, and if possible, it would be mischievous and undesirable, to try to break up all combinations merely because they are large and successful, and to put the business of the country back into the middle of the eighteenth century conditions of intense and unregulated competition between small and weak business concerns. Such an effort represents not progressiveness but an unintelligent though doubtless entirely well-meaning toryism. Moreover, the effort to administer a law merely by lawsuits and court decisions is bound to end in signal failure, and meanwhile to be attended with delays and uncertainties, and to put a premium upon legal sharp practice. Such an effort does not adequately punish the guilty, and yet works great harm to the innocent. Moreover, it entirely fails to give the publicity which is one of the best by-products of the system of control by administrative officials; publicity, which is not only good in itself, but furnishes the data for whatever further action may be necessary. We need to formulate immediately and definitely a policy which, in dealing with big corporations that behave themselves and which contain no menace save what is necessarily potential in any corporation which is of great size and very well managed, shall aim not at their destruction but at their regulation and supervision, so that the Government shall control them in such fashion as amply to safeguard the interests of the whole public, including producers, consumers, and wage-workers. This control should, if necessary, be pushed in extreme cases to the point of exercising control over mo-

nopoly prices, as rates on railways are now controlled; although this is not a power that should be used when it is possible to avoid it. The law should be clear, unambiguous, certain, so that honest men may not find that unwittingly they have violated it. In short, our aim should be, not to destroy, but effectively and in thoroughgoing fashion to regulate and control, in the public interest, the great instrumentalities of modern business, which it is destructive of the general welfare of the community to destroy, and which nevertheless it is vitally necessary to that general welfare to regulate and control. Competition will remain as a very important factor when once we have destroyed the unfair business methods, the criminal interference with the rights of others, which alone enabled certain swollen combinations to crush out their competitors — and, incidentally, the "conservatives" will do well to remember that these unfair and iniquitous methods by great masters of corporate capital have done more to cause popular discontent with the propertied classes than all the orations of all the Socialist orators in the country put together.

Woodrow Wilson: MONOPOLY OR OPPORTUNITY?

A TRUST is formed in this way: a few gentlemen "promote" it — that is to say, they get it up, being given enormous fees for their kindness, which fees are loaded on to the undertaking in the form

of securities of one kind or another. The argument of the promoters is, not that every one who comes into the combination can carry on his business more efficiently than he did before; the argument

From *The New Freedom* by Woodrow Wilson. Copyright 1913 by Doubleday and Company, Inc. Reprinted by permission.

is: we will assign to you as your share in the pool twice, three times, four times, or five times what you could have sold your business for to an individual competitor who would have to run it on an economic and competitive basis. We can afford to buy it at such a figure because we are shutting out competition. We can afford to make the stock of the combination half a dozen times what it naturally would be and pay dividends on it, because there will be nobody to dispute the prices we shall fix.

Talk of that as sound business? Talk of that as inevitable? It is based upon nothing except power. It is not based upon efficiency. It is no wonder that the big trusts are not prospering in proportion to such competitors as they still have in such parts of their business as competitors have access to; they are prospering freely only in those fields to which competition has no access. Read the statistics of the Steel Trust, if you don't believe it. Read the statistics of any trust. They are constantly nervous about competition, and they are constantly buying up new competitors in order to narrow the field. The United States Steel Corporation is gaining in its supremacy in the American market only with regard to the cruder manufactures of iron and steel, but wherever, as in the field of more advanced manufactures of iron and steel, it has important competitors, its portion of the product is not increasing, but is decreasing, and its competitors, where they have a foothold, are often more efficient than it is.

Why? Why, with unlimited capital and innumerable mines and plants everywhere in the United States, can't they beat the other fellows in the market? Partly because they are carrying too much. Partly because they are unwieldy. Their organization is imperfect. They bought up inefficient plants along with efficient, and they have got to carry what they have paid for, even if they have to shut some of the plants up in order to make any interest on their investments; or, rather, not interest on their investments, because that is an incorrect word — on their alleged capitalization. Here we have a lot of giants staggering along under an almost intolerable weight of artificial burdens, which they have put on their own backs, and constantly looking about lest some little pigmy with a round stone in a sling may come out and slay them.

For my part, I want the pigmy to have a chance to come out. And I foresee a time when the pigmies will be so much more athletic, so much more astute, so much more active, than the giants, that it will be a case of Jack the giant-killer. Just let some of the youngsters I know have a chance and they'll give these gentlemen points. Lend them a little money. They can't get any now. See to it that when they have got a local market they can't be squeezed out of it. Give them a chance to capture that market and then see them capture another one and another one, until these men who are carrying an intolerable load of artificial securities find that they have got to get down to hard pan to keep their foothold at all. I am willing to let Jack come into the field with the giant, and if Jack has the brains that some Jacks that I know in America have, then I should like to see the giant get the better of him, with the load that he, the giant, has to carry — the load of water. For I'll undertake to put a waterlogged giant out of business any time, if you will give me a fair field and as much credit as I am entitled to, and let the law do what from time immemorial law has been expected to do — see fair play.

As for watered stock, I know all the sophistical arguments, and they are many, for capitalizing earning capacity. It is a very attractive and interesting argument, and in some instances it is legitimately used. But there is a line you cross, above which you are not capitalizing your earning capacity, but capitalizing your control of the market, capitalizing the profits which you got by your control of the market, and didn't get by efficiency and economy. These things are not hidden even from the layman. These are not half-hidden from college men. The college men's days of innocence have passed, and their days of sophistication have come. They know what is going on, because we live in a talkative world, full of statistics, full of congressional inquiries, full of trials of persons who have attempted to live independently of the statutes of the United States; and so a great many things have come to light under oath, which we must believe upon the credibility of the witnesses who are, indeed, in many instances very eminent and respectable witnesses.

I take my stand absolutely, where every progressive ought to take his stand, on the proposition that private monopoly is indefensible and intolerable. And there I will fight my battle. And I know how to fight it. Everybody who has even read the newspapers knows the means by which these men built up their power and created these monopolies. Any decently equipped lawyer can suggest to you statutes by which the whole business can be stopped. What these gentlemen do not want is this: they do not want to be compelled to meet all comers on equal terms. I am perfectly willing that they should beat any competitor by fair means; but I know the foul means they have adopted, and I know that they can be stopped by law. If they think that

coming into the market upon the basis of mere efficiency, upon the mere basis of knowing how to manufacture goods better than anybody else and to sell them cheaper than anybody else, they can carry the immense amount of water that they have put into their enterprises in order to buy up rivals, then they are perfectly welcome to try it. But there must be no squeezing out of the beginner, no crippling his credit; no discrimination against retailers who buy from a rival; no threats against concerns who sell supplies to a rival; no holding back of raw material from him; no secret arrangements against him. All the fair competition you choose, but no unfair competition of any kind. And then when unfair competition is eliminated, let us see these gentlemen carry their tanks of water on their backs. All that I ask and all I shall fight for is that they shall come into the field against merit and brains everywhere. If they can beat other American brains, then they have got the best brains.

But if you want to know how far brains go, as things now are, suppose you try to match your better wares against these gentlemen, and see them undersell you before your market is any bigger than the locality and make it absolutely impossible for you to get a fast foothold. If you want to know how brains count, originate some invention which will improve the kind of machinery they are using, and then see if you can borrow enough money to manufacture it. You may be offered something for your patent by the corporation — which will perhaps lock it up in a safe and go on using the old machinery; but you will not be allowed to manufacture. I know men who have tried it, and they could not get the money, because the great money lenders of this country are in the arrangement with the great manufacturers of this country, and they do not propose to see their control of the market interfered with by outsiders. And who are outsiders? Why, all the rest of the people of the United States are outsiders.

They are rapidly making us outsiders with respect even of the things that come from the bosom of the earth, and which belong to us in a peculiar sense. Certain monopolies in this country have gained almost complete control of the raw material, chiefly in the mines, out of which the great body of manufactures are carried on, and they now discriminate, when they will, in the sale of that raw material between those who are rivals of the monopoly and those who submit to the monopoly. We must soon come to the point where we shall say to the men who own these essentials of industry that they have got to part with these essentials by sale to all citizens of the United States with the same readiness and upon the same terms. Or else we shall tie up the resources of this country under private control in such fashion as will make our independent development absolutely impossible.

There is another injustice that monopoly engages in. The trust that deals in the cruder products which are to be transformed into the more elaborate manufactures often will not sell these crude products except upon the terms of monopoly — that is to say, the people that deal with them must buy exclusively from them. And so again you have the lines of development tied up and the connections of development knotted and fastened so that you cannot wrench them apart.

Again, the manufacturing monopolies are so interlaced in their personal relationships with the great shipping interests of this country, and with the great railroads, that they can often largely determine the rates of shipment.

The people of this country are being very subtly dealt with. You know, of course, that, unless our Commerce Commissions are absolutely sleepless, you can get rebates without calling them such at all. The most complicated study I know of is the classification of freight by the railway company. If I wanted to make a special rate on a special thing, all I should have to do is to put it in a special class in the freight classification, and the trick is done. And when you reflect that the twenty-four men who control the United States Steel Corporation, for example, are either presidents or vice-presidents or directors in 55 per cent of the railways of the United States, reckoning by the valuation of those railroads and the amount of their stocks and bonds, you know just how close the whole thing is knitted together in our industrial system, and how great the temptation is. These twenty-four gentlemen administer that corporation as if it belonged to them. The amazing thing to me is that the people of the United States have not seen that the administration of a great business like that is not a private affair; it is a public affair.

I have been told by a great many men that the idea I have, that by restoring competition you can restore industrial freedom, is based upon a failure to observe the actual happenings of the last decades in this country; because, they say, it is just free competition that has made it possible for the big to crush the little.

I reply, it is not free competition that has done that; it is illicit competition. It is competition of the kind that the law ought to stop, and can stop — this crushing of the little man.

You know, of course, how the little man is crushed by the trusts. He gets a

local market. The big concerns come in
and undersell him in his local market,
and that is the only market he has; if he
cannot make a profit there, he is killed.
They can make a profit all through the
rest of the Union, while they are underselling him in his locality, and recouping
themselves by what they can earn elsewhere. Thus their competitors can be put
out of business, one by one, wherever
they dare to show a head. Inasmuch as
they rise up only one by one, these big
concerns can see to it that new competitors never come into the larger field. You
have to begin somewhere. You can't begin in space. You can't begin in an air-
ship. You have got to begin in some
community. Your market has got to be
your neighbors first and those who know
you there. But unless you have unlimited
capital (which of course you wouldn't
have when you were beginning) or unlimited credit (which these gentlemen
can see to it that you shan't get), they
can kill you out in your local market any
time they try, on the same basis exactly
as that on which they beat organized
labor; for they can sell at a loss in your
market because they are selling at a
profit everywhere else, and they can re-
coup the losses by which they beat you
by the profits which they make in fields
where they have beaten other fellows
and put them out. If ever a competitor
who by good luck has plenty of money
does break into the wider market, then
the trust has to buy him out, paying
three or four times what the business is
worth. Following such a purchase it has
got to pay the interest on the price it has
paid for the business, and it has got to
tax the whole people of the United States,
in order to pay the interest on what it
borrowed to do that, or on the stocks and
bonds it issued to do it with. Therefore
the big trusts, the big combinations, are

the most wasteful, the most uneconomi-
cal, and, after they pass a certain size,
the most inefficient, way of conducting
the industries of this country.

A notable example is the way in which
Mr. Carnegie was bought out of the steel
business. Mr. Carnegie could build better mills and make better steel rails and
make them cheaper than anybody else
connected with what afterward became
the United States Steel Corporation.
They didn't dare leave him outside. He
had so much more brains in finding out
the best processes; he had so much more
shrewdness in surrounding himself with
the most successful assistants; he knew
so well when a young man who came
into his employ was fit for promotion
and was ripe to put at the head of some
branch of his business and was sure to
make good, that he could undersell every
mother's son of them in the market for
steel rails. And they bought him out at
a price that amounted to three or four
times — I believe actually five times —
the estimated value of his properties and
of his business, because they couldn't
beat him in competition. And then in
what they charged afterward for their
product — the product of his mills included — they made us pay the interest
on the four or five times the difference.

That is the difference between a big
business and a trust. A trust is an arrangement to get rid of competition, and
a big business is a business that has survived competition by conquering in the
field of intelligence and economy. A trust
does not bring efficiency to the aid of
business; it *buys efficiency out of business.* I am for big business, and I am
against the trusts. Any man who can sur-
vive by his brains, any man who can put
the others out of the business by making the thing cheaper to the consumer
at the same time that he is increasing its

intrinsic value and quality, I take off my hat to, and I say: "You are the man who can build up the United States, and I wish there were more of you.". . .

The doctrine that monopoly is inevitable and that the only course open to the people of the United States is to submit to and regulate it found a champion during the campaign of 1912 in the new party, or branch of the Republican party, founded under the leadership of Mr. Roosevelt, with the conspicuous aid — I mention him with no satirical intention, but merely to set the facts down accurately — of Mr. George W. Perkins, organizer of the Steel Trust and the Harvester Trust, and with the support of more than three millions of citizens, many of them among the most patriotic, conscientious and high-minded men and women of the land. The fact that its acceptance of monopoly was a feature of the new party platform from which the attention of the generous and just was diverted by the charm of a social program of great attractiveness to all concerned for the amelioration of the lot of those who suffer wrong and privation, and the further fact that, even so, the platform was repudiated by the majority of the nation, render it no less necessary to reflect on the significance of the confession made for the first time by any party in the country's history. It may be useful, in order to relieve the minds of many from an error of no small magnitude, to consider now, the heat of a presidential contest being past, exactly what it was that Mr. Roosevelt proposed.

Mr. Roosevelt attached to his platform some very splendid suggestions as to noble enterprises which we ought to undertake for the uplift of the human race; but when I hear an ambitious platform put forth, I am very much more interested in the dynamics of it than in the rhetoric of it. I have a very practical mind, and I want to know who are going to do those things and how they are going to be done. If you have read the trust plank in that platform as often as I have read it, you have found it very long, but very tolerant. It did not anywhere condemn monopoly, except in words; its essential meaning was that the trusts have been bad and must be made to be good. You know that Mr. Roosevelt long ago classified trusts for us as good and bad, and he said that he was afraid only of the bad ones. Now he does not desire that there should be any more bad ones, but proposes that they should all be made good by discipline, directly applied by a commission of executive appointment. All he explicitly complains of is lack of publicity and lack of fairness; not the exercise of power, for throughout that plank the power of the great corporations is accepted as the inevitable consequence of the modern organization of industry. All that it is proposed to do is to take them under control and regulation. The national administration having for sixteen years been virtually under the regulation of the trusts, it would be merely a family matter were the parts reversed and were the other members of the family to exercise the regulation. And the trusts, apparently, which might, in such circumstances, comfortably continue to administer our affairs under the mollifying influences of the federal government, would then, if you please, be the instrumentalities by which all the humanistic, benevolent program of the rest of that interesting platform would be carried out!

I have read and reread that plank, so as to be sure that I get it right. All that it complains of is — and the complaint is a just one, surely — that these gentlemen exercise their power in a way that is secret. Therefore, we must have publicity. Sometimes they are arbitrary; therefore they need regulation. Sometimes they do not consult the general interests of the community; therefore they need to be reminded of those general interests by an industrial commission. But at every turn it is the trusts who are to do us good, and not we ourselves.

Again, I absolutely protest against being put into the hands of trustees. Mr. Roosevelt's conception of government is Mr. Taft's conception, that the Presidency of the United States is the presidency of a board of directors. I am willing to admit that if the people of the United States cannot get justice for themselves, then it is high time that they should join the third party and get it from somebody else. The justice proposed is very beautiful; it is very attractive; there were planks in that platform which stir all the sympathies of the heart; they proposed things that we all want to do; but the question is, Who is going to do them? Through whose instrumentality? Are Americans ready to ask the trusts to give us in pity what we ought, in justice, to take?

The third party says that the present system of our industry and trade has come to stay. Mind you, these artificially built up things, these things that can't maintain themselves in the market without monopoly, have come to stay, and the only thing that the government can do, the only thing that the third party proposes should be done, is to set up a commission to regulate them. It accepts them. It says: "We will not undertake, it were futile to undertake, to prevent monopoly, but we will go into an arrangement by which we will make these monopolies kind to you. We will guarantee that they shall be pitiful. We will guarantee that they shall pay the right wages.

We will guarantee that they shall do everything kind and public-spirited, which they have never heretofore shown the least inclination to do."

Don't you realize that that is a blind alley? You can't find your way to liberty that way. You can't find your way to social reform through the forces that have made social reform necessary.

The fundamental part of such a program is that the trusts shall be recognized as a permanent part of our economic order, and that the government shall try to make trusts the ministers, the instruments, through which the life of this country shall be justly and happily developed on its industrial side. Now, everything that touches our lives sooner or later goes back to the industries which sustain our lives. I have often reflected that there is a very human order in the petitions in our Lord's prayer. For we pray first of all, "Give us this day our daily bread," knowing that it is useless to pray for spiritual graces on an empty stomach, and that the amount of wages we get, the kind of clothes we wear, the kind of food we can afford to buy, is fundamental to everything else.

Those who administer our physical life, therefore, administer our spiritual life; and if we are going to carry out the fine purpose of that great chorus which supporters of the third party sang almost with religious fervor, then we have got to find out through whom these purposes of humanity are going to be realized. It is a mere enterprise, so far as that part of it is concerned, of making the monopolies philanthropic.

I do not want to live under a philanthropy. I do not want to be taken care of by the government, either directly, or by any instruments through which the government is acting. I want only to have right and justice prevail, so far as

I am concerned. Give me right and justice and I will undertake to take care of myself. If you enthrone the trusts as the means of the development of this country under the supervision of the government, then I shall pray the old Spanish proverb, "God save me from my friends, and I'll take care of my enemies." Because I want to be saved from these friends. Observe that I say these friends, for I am ready to admit that a great many men who believe that the development of industry in this country through monopolies is inevitable intend to be the friends of the people. Though they profess to be my friends, they are undertaking a way of friendship which renders it impossible that they should do me the fundamental service that I demand — namely, that I should be free and should have the same opportunities that everybody else has.

For I understand it to be the fundamental proposition of American liberty that we do not desire special privilege, because we know special privilege will never comprehend the general welfare. This is the fundamental, spiritual difference between adherents of the party now about to take charge of the government and those who have been in charge of it in recent years. They are so indoctrinated with the idea that only the big business interests of this country understand the United States and can make it prosperous that they cannot divorce their thoughts from that obsession. They have put the government into the hands of trustees, and Mr. Taft and Mr. Roosevelt were the rival candidates to preside over the board of trustees. They were candidates to serve the people, no doubt, to the best of their ability, but it was not their idea to serve them directly; they proposed to serve them indirectly through the enormous forces already set up, which are so great that there is almost an open question whether the government of the United States with the people back of it is strong enough to overcome and rule them.

Shall we try to get the grip of monopoly away from our lives, or shall we not? Shall we withhold our hand and say monopoly is inevitable, that all that we can do is to regulate it? Shall we say that all that we can do is to put government in competition with monopoly and try its strength against it? Shall we admit that the creature of our own hands is stronger than we are? We have been dreading all along the time when the combined power of high finance would be greater than the power of the government. Have we come to a time when the President of the United States or any man who wishes to be the President must doff his cap in the presence of this high finance, and say, "You are our inevitable master, but we will see how we can make the best of it?"

We are at the parting of the ways. We have, not one or two or three, but many, established and formidable monopolies in the United States. We have, not one or two, but many, fields of endeavor into which it is difficult, if not impossible, for the independent man to enter. We have restricted credit, we have restricted opportunity, we have controlled development, and we have come to be one of the worst ruled, one of the most completely controlled and dominated, governments in the civilized world — no longer a government by free opinion, no longer a government by conviction and the vote of the majority, but a government by the opinion and the duress of small groups of dominant men.

If the government is to tell big business men how to run their business, then don't you see that big business men have to get closer to the government even than they are now? Don't you see that they must capture the government, in order not to be restrained too much by it? Must capture the government? They have already captured it. Are you going to invite those inside to stay inside? They don't have to get there. They are there. Are you going to own your own premises, or are you not? That is your choice. Are you going to say: "You didn't get into the house the right way, but you are in there, God bless you; we will stand out here in the cold and you can hand us out something once in a while?"

At the least, under the plan I am opposing, there will be an avowed partnership between the government and the trusts. I take it that the firm will be ostensibly controlled by the senior member. For I take it that the government of the United States is at least the senior member, though the younger member has all along been running the business. But when all the momentum, when all the energy, when a great deal of the genius, as so often happens in partnerships the world over, is with the junior partner, I don't think that the superintendence of the senior partner is going to amount to very much. And I don't believe that benevolence can be read into the hearts of the trusts by the superintendence and suggestions of the federal government; because the government has never within my recollection had its suggestions accepted by the trusts. On the contrary, the suggestions of the trusts have been accepted by the government.

There is no hope to be seen for the people of the United States until the partnership is dissolved. And the business of the party now entrusted with power is going to be to dissolve it.

Those who supported the third party supported, I believe, a program perfectly agreeable to the monopolies. How those who have been fighting monopoly through all their career can reconcile the continuation of the battle under the banner of the very men they have been fighting, I cannot imagine. I challenge the program in its fundamentals as not a progressive program at all. Why did Mr. Gary suggest this very method when he was at the head of the Steel Trust? Why is this very method commended here, there, and everywhere by the men who are interested in the maintenance of the present economic system of the United States? Why do the men who do not wish to be disturbed urge the adoption of this program? The rest of the program is very handsome; there is beating in it a great pulse of sympathy for the human race. But I do not want the sympathy of the trusts for the human race. I do not want their condescending assistance.

And I warn every progressive Republican that by lending his assistance to this program he is playing false to the very cause in which he had enlisted. That cause was a battle against monopoly, against control, against the concentration of power in our economic development, against all those things that interfere with absolutely free enterprise. I believe that some day these gentlemen will wake up and realize that they have misplaced their trust, not in an individual, it may be, but in a program which is fatal to the things we hold dearest.

If there is any meaning in the things I have been urging, it is this: that the incubus that lies upon this country is the present monopolistic organization of our industrial life. That is the thing which certain Republicans became "insurgents" in order to throw off. And yet some of them allowed themselves to be so misled as to go into the camp of the third party in order to remove what the third party proposed to legalize. My point is that this is a method conceived from the point of view of the very men who are to be controlled, and that this is just the wrong point of view from which to conceive it.

I said not long ago that Mr. Roosevelt was promoting a plan for the control of monopoly which was supported by the United States Steel Corporation. Mr. Roosevelt denied that he was being supported by more than one member of that corporation. He was thinking of money. I was thinking of ideas. I did not say that he was getting money from these gentlemen; it was a matter of indifference to me where he got his money; but it was a matter of a great deal of difference to me where he got his ideas. He got his idea with regard to the regulation of monopoly from the gentlemen who form the United States Steel Corporation. I am perfectly ready to admit that the gentlemen who control the United States Steel Corporation have a perfect right to entertain their own ideas about this and to urge them upon the people of the United States; but I want to say that their ideas are not my ideas; and I am perfectly certain that they would not promote any idea which interfered with their monopoly. Inasmuch, therefore, as I hope and intend to interfere with monopoly just as much as possible, I cannot subscribe to arrangements by which they know that it will not be disturbed.

The Roosevelt plan is that there shall be an industrial commission charged with the supervision of the great monopolistic combinations which have been formed under the protection of the tariff, and that the government of the United States shall see to it that these gentlemen who have conquered labor shall be kind to labor. I find, then, the proposition to be this: That there shall be two masters, the great corporation, and over it the government of the United States; and I ask who is going to be master of the government of the United States? It has a master now — those who in combination control these monopolies. And if the government controlled by the monopolies in its turn controls the monopolies, the partnership is finally consummated.

I don't care how benevolent the master is going to be, I will not live under a master. That is not what America was created for. America was created in order that every man should have the same chance as every other man to exercise mastery over his own fortunes. What I want to do is analogous to what the authorities of the city of Glasgow did with tenement houses. I want to light and patrol the corridors of these great organizations in order to see that nobody who tries to traverse them is waylaid and maltreated. If you will but hold off the adversaries, if you will but see to it that the weak are protected, I will venture a wager with you that there are some men in the United States, now weak, economically weak, who have brains enough to compete with these gentlemen and who will presently come into the market and put these gentlemen on their mettle. And the minute they come into the market there will be a bigger market for labor and a different wage scale for labor. . . .

Hearings before the Committee on Investigation of the United States Steel Corporation

62 CONGRESS, 2 SESSION (1912)

A. *Testimony of Elbert H. Gary, Chairman of the Board, United States Steel Corporation*

THE CHAIRMAN. Judge, at the close of the last meeting I asked you something concerning the Iron and Steel Institute, and called your attention to an editorial in the Ironmonger. If you have any statement to make in reference to that you can make it now.

MR. GARY. Mr. Chairman, the question, as it seems to me, opens up a consideration of what has been referred to as proceedings at some of the dinners, as well as a proposed international iron and steel institute; and with the permission of the committee I will endeavor to state, as briefly as I can, exactly what is involved in the whole subject matter, intending to show what we have done and what our intentions have been and are.

The chairman inquired yesterday whether or not representatives of the press were admitted to the dinners, and I answered in the negative, except as to the editors of three of the trade journals. The real reason for not making it an open meeting is found in the fact that there is always more or less risk of a misstatement of exactly what occurred, unless the representatives are thoroughly familiar with the subject matter. For instance, it was published in one of the papers this morning that the witness on the stand yesterday admitted that the United States Steel Corporation was dominant, or in control of the domestic steel business of this country. Of course that was not intended as a misstatement; but it did not represent the facts, and whoever wrote it supposed that because the United States Steel Corporation was admitted to be dominant as to the subsidiary companies of the United States Steel Corporation that, therefore, it admitted it controlled the whole business of this country — very far from the fact. I am not making any complaint, but nevertheless there is always that danger.

As a matter of fact, the United States Steel Corporation at the time it was organized had about 60 per cent of the steel business of this country, and at present has about 50 per cent of the domestic steel business of this country, as I am prepared to show you by the figures in detail, if you care to know, later.

Now, at the time of the panic in New York there was, of course, great demoralization temporarily in business, and the fear existed that that would be spread and might be prolonged. The iron and steel industry has been recognized as one of the leading barometers of trade, and it was believed by many people of prominence to be equally important, if practicable, to prevent a great demoralization in the steel trade. Moreover, many of the leading jobbers, so called, throughout the country were possessed of large quantities of material which they had purchased for resale, and if the prices of those commodities should be materially reduced, of course the inventories of those gentlemen would be materially marked down, their banks would call upon them for the payment of loans, and in many cases at least it was believed there would be failures and bankruptcies, and if such conditions were brought about it seemed to be the consensus of opinion that the panic would be long continued.

Now, I need not suggest to lawyers, at least on the committee, and perhaps you are all lawyers, I do not know about that, that the interpretation of the Sherman Act has been more or less involved in doubt. Evidently the act was intended to prevent the existence and exercise of monopolies and also the restraint of trade. A company like the United States Steel Corporation, with 50 per cent of the domestic steel business of this country, was confronted with two propositions. It had no right to endeavor to prevent reductions in prices, or, in other words, to maintain the equilibrium of business and maintain prices substantially level or at least free from sudden and violent fluctuations by means of any sort of an agreement express or implied. We had no lawful right, as I understand, to make any agreement, express or implied, directly or indirectly, with our competitors in business to maintain prices, notwithstanding we were receiving letters daily from the jobbers all over the country begging us, if possible, to prevent demoralization and to prevent decrease in prices which should mark down their inventories and in many cases subject them to the risk of bankruptcy. On the other hand, considering this same question of sustaining, so far as practicable,

the equilibrium of trade, we believed we had no moral or legal right to become involved in a bitter and destructive competition, such as used to follow any kind of depression in business among the iron and steel manufacturers, for the reason that if we should go into a competition of that kind it meant a war of the survival of the fittest; it meant that a large percentage, as in old times, of the people engaged in the manufacture of steel would be forced into bankruptcy for many reasons — their facilities for manufacture were not so good, their cost of production was high, their equipment, their organization, their decreased ownership of some of the raw products and other things of that kind which enter into the cost of production, would place them at a disadvantage, and therefore it was believed, by me at least, that it was not for the best interests of the manufacturers generally or for their customers who desired stability as opposed to demoralization and wide fluctuations or for the employees of the various corporations throughout the country who desired, so far as possible, steady work — continuous work at the best prices, and a wide, sudden, extreme lowering of prices necessarily meant reduction in the wages. Reductions were advocated almost at the start of the panic of 1907, and many of you know that our company took a leading part in opposing that and we went through that panic without making any reduction in wages, although many, if not all, of our competitors before the year was terminated did materially reduce their wages.

Now, the question was how to get between the two extremes of securing a monopoly by driving out competition, however good-naturedly, in a bitter, destructive competition or without making any agreement, express or implied, tacit or otherwise, which should result in the maintenance of prices, and so, gentlemen, I invited a large percentage of the steel interests of the country to meet me at dinner and then presented these views to them and, so far as I could, the results of our becoming demoralized and extreme decreases in prices like those which obtained under the old regime. Then, I said that it seemed to me the only way we could lawfully prevent such demoralization and maintain a reasonable steadiness in business, whether we lowered the prices from time to time or not, whether depending upon circumstances we were willing to make concessions or reductions after the jobbers had relieved themselves of the large lots, so as to prevent demoralization, was for the steel people to come together occasionally and to tell one to the others exactly what his business was. In other words, a disclosure by each one to all others of all the circumstances surrounding his particular business. In other words, to state it simply, if three men, gentlemen on this committee, were practicing law in a certain town and each one knew that the customary fee for services in court was $50 a day and a gentleman from another part of the country should locate in that town and make a totally different price, very much lower, he would immediately get up some sort of competition amongst these professional men. If those three men, however, on this committee, were in daily conference and each one knew that the others did not propose to change the fees, probably this outsider would not make very much headway in creating a demoralization.

Mr. BARTLETT. I do not think your illustration is very apt, because the lawyers do not furnish the same kind of finished material as those engaged in the manufacture of steel.

MR. GARY. Of course, it only applies so far as it comes within the views which I have stated, which assumed that it had been the established practice of the three lawyers I suggested to charge that price as a reasonable price. That, of course, is a very crude illustration, but I think it makes the point.

MR. BARTLETT. It has been a long time since there has been any effort anywhere to control the fees of lawyers. There was a time in England when it was not only not permitted, but was prohibited.

MR. GARY. You can not control the fees of the lawyers and you can not control the prices of steel in the way I have suggested. We have never controlled the prices and we never mean to control the prices, and we do not expect to in that way; but we have by this interchange of information prevented the demoralization which otherwise would have resulted. We have not done more because we could not do more.

You know, for instance, that last week — I think it was last week — one of the manufacturers of iron and steel made sudden cuts in their prices, and of course the others had to follow. Whether it was wise to make them at that time I do not know. Personally, I have never stood for unchanged or unchangeable prices. I do not believe in that. I believe the price under no circumstances should be above what is reasonable and fair.

THE CHAIRMAN. If I apprehend you there, taking that statement with your previous statement, you believe that prices should be subject to change not through the external exigencies of trade or through natural or unnatural conditions, such as panics and the like, that they ought not to absolutely control prices, but that prices should change through the common consent and the kindly concurrence of the men most interested in those prices?

MR. GARY. No; your statement is all right until you come to the last part.

THE CHAIRMAN. I may have misunderstood you.

MR. GARY. I do not believe in the change by common consent. I do not believe you have a right to do that, but I do believe that if one individual is possessed of information concerning the conditions surrounding the other's business that it prevents many times, and perhaps in most cases, the extreme, the unreasonable, the bitter, and destructive competition which used to exist. Not only that, I believe it prevents the increases of prices.

I am very sure the committee is aware of the fact that it has been an effort of the United States Steel Corporation always to prevent an unreasonable or sudden increase of price of its commodities. The old way of doing business was for the man who had a purse big enough to go into the trade and keep his mills full regardless of the effect it had on other mills throughout the country. If he could not sell at a profit, he sold at cost or below cost temporarily. He made it certain that his mills were kept running all the time, whether or not the result was to drive all his competitors entirely out of business. That is why there would be so many failures in the iron and steel business. Then, on the other hand, at times when the demand was very great and the customers were willing to pay almost any price to get prompt deliveries he would take advantage of that and put his price up as high as the trade would stand. I do not believe that is for the best interests of the country. I do not believe it is for the best interests of the consumer. I know the consumers do not like that. It is not for the best interests of the employees, and it is not for the best interests of the general business conditions. Stability, so far as it is practicable, is a thing often needed.

THE CHAIRMAN. I do not wish to interrupt the witness, but there is one statement that is surprising to me, and that is this obstinate hostility of the consumer to a reduction in prices.

MR. GARY. You have stated it perhaps different.

THE CHAIRMAN. Too strong?

MR. GARY. I think you have.

THE CHAIRMAN. I was surprised, although I may have misunderstood you. You spoke of the consumer objecting to fluctuations in prices, in which event he would have to object to a fall as well as a rise?

MR. GARY. I think any of us would rather have the prices of our tailor or our grocer substantially uniform, assuming they are fair and reasonable, year in and year out, than to have the prices very low in the time of panic and depression and then in other times very high and unreasonable. I think what the customer prefers is to have reasonable stability of prices. For instance, a man is desirous of putting up a steel building, and he finds the price of steel $30 a ton. If he thinks that is a reasonable price, he is perfectly willing to pay it unless he knows by experience or fear that next week another man can go to the same producer or some other producer and buy the same material 30 per cent cheaper, which would enable his competitor to put up a cheaper building and unduly compete with him in renting the building.

When the business is conducted in

the way it used to be conducted, very frequently some of the men engaged in trade take advantage of the necessities of a competitor and suddenly and unduly drop the prices and drive him out of business. That has been resorted to. The customer does not like that, as a rule. He wants to know what he can depend upon.

I do not hesitate to say, Mr. Chairman, in connection with your suggestion, what I said two or three years before in appearing before a congressional committee. I realize as fully, I think, as this committee that it is very important to consider how the people shall be protected against imposition or oppression as the possible result of great aggregations of capital, whether in the possession of corporations or individuals. I believe that is a very important question, and personally I believe that the Sherman Act does not meet and will never fully prevent that. I believe we must come to enforced publicity and governmental control.

MR. YOUNG. You mean governmental control of prices?

MR. GARY. I do; even as to prices, and, so far as I am concerned, speaking for our company, so far as I have the right, I would be very glad if we knew exactly where we stand, if we could be freed from danger, trouble, and criticism by the public, and if we had some place where we could go, to a responsible governmental authority, and say to them, "Here are our facts and figures, here is our property, here our cost of produc-

tion; now you tell us what we have the right to do and what prices we have the right to charge." I know that is a very extreme view, and I know that the railroads objected to it for a long time; but whether the mere standpoint of making the most money is concerned or not, whether it is the wise thing, I believe it is the necessary thing, and it seems to me corporations have no right to disregard these public questions and these public interests.

MR. LITTLETON. Is it your position that cooperation is bound to take the place of competition?

MR. GARY. It is my position.

MR. LITTLETON. And that cooperation therefore requires strict governmental supervision?

MR. GARY. That is a very good statement of the case. I believe that thoroughly.

MR. LITTLETON. Is it your position that the Sherman antitrust law recently interpreted by the court nevertheless leaves an archaic law to deal with the modern situation?

MR. GARY. It is.

MR. LITTLETON. It is your position that that practically orders a continuance of the old warfare of competition?

MR. GARY. I am afraid it does. I do not know that it does, but I fear it does. I know by your questions that you realize the position we occupy, the position we do not wish to occupy. We do not want to be dealing in uncertainty, groping around in darkness, not knowing what we have the right to do.

B. *Testimony of Andrew Carnegie*

MR. GARDNER. Mr. Carnegie, just to clear up this subject, I want to make this statement first and then you will see what I am driving at:

There are two lines of thought developing in this country amongst the people who think that the present state of affairs in large industries, or, as people now call them, large units of production, needs some change.

There is the line of thought which perhaps I could express best by President Taft's message, which believes that dissolution of large units should go on under the existing Sherman law. There is a line of thought which I can best express by calling it the one indicated by ex-President Roosevelt in the Outlook article, which looks to the recognition of large units, but their control by a court or commission such as you are asking for.

Do you follow me up to that point?

MR. CARNEGIE. Certainly, Mr. Gardner.

MR. GARDNER. In which class of mind do you find yourself?

MR. CARNEGIE. Mr. Gardner, I, of course, am familiar with Mr. Roosevelt's position, and I have heard from him on the subject and have agreed with him.

I think that, for the present, you should allow large organizations to continue and you should pass what we recommend — this law for a commission to fix maximum prices. That is a step in the right direction.

If you will be patient we shall see whether that needs any further legislation, and, if so, we shall make it. Your successors will make it if you do not. They will have all the facts before them, which we have not.

In taking a new path I would only go to the first resting place and sit there and await results. And I hope you will agree with me in that, and that we should not assume what will happen from this legislation until we give it a trial. I hope you will agree with that.

MR. GARDNER. Your present idea, Mr. Carnegie, is that, for the present at least, we should travel in the direction of the recognition, by Government control over large units, such as the same direction which we have taken with regard to railroad corporations?

MR. CARNEGIE. Certainly. Do you agree with that? I would like very much to know.

MR. GARDNER. I have not altogether made up my mind. I will be perfectly frank. I shall give indications in this colloquy — because I shall not call it an examination — of the way my mind is working.

* * *

MR. GARDNER. Let me ask you this question, to elucidate these two directions:

In the first place, if dissolution takes place by the order of the courts, either under the imperfect law which we have at present or under the law made much more severe, in your opinion will that lessen the cost of steel products to the people, other things being equal?

MR. CARNEGIE. No, sir. My court, that I stand for, would take care of the rights of the people; and, Judge — I always think of you as a judge or a lawyer —

MR. GARDNER. I was a bookkeeper. (Laughter.)

MR. CARNEGIE. I am delighted to hear such an exposition. Your mind has traveled exactly over the same ground that mine has in studying this question.

Wherein we differ is this: You are not sure that it is necessary to dissolve these large companies. You are not sure.

Mr. Gardner, you are sure about one thing, that they must not be permitted to charge monopolistic prices, as they have been doing, by agreements among themselves. You are sure about that?

MR. GARDNER. Wait a moment, Mr. Carnegie. I have my own opinion as to the question of the agreements amongst themselves, that I am not willing, without further evidence, to express, but I will say this: I ought not to answer your question as to whether I think that they are charging excessive prices or not now. I do not think I would have the right to give anything more than general conclusions, so I shall not contradict you.

MR. CARNEGIE. But wait. Suppose you assume, for the moment, that they are doing so.

MR. GARDNER. Yes.

MR. CARNEGIE. What would your position be? Suppose, for the moment, they are doing so.

MR. GARDNER. Yes.

MR. CARNEGIE. What would your position be?

MR. GARDNER. My position would be that we must travel in one of those two directions; preferably, that we ought to travel in the direction which produces the lowest prices ultimately, even though it appears to be a step in the direction of socialism.

MR. CARNEGIE. Then do not let us discuss that. My view is that the agent of the Republic on that proposed commission will take good care about prices.

MR. GARDNER. I quite agree with you.

MR. CARNEGIE. Then, if you agree upon that, there can be no doubt that you and I shake hands, and if I were a Congressman today with you, you and I would vote together for the establishment of that commission.

MR. GARDNER. That may not be at all the question which presents itself.

MR. CARNEGIE. I am assuming that it did. Then we would be together.

MR. GARDNER. I think you have a little bit gotten away from what I want to get at. I want to get at two great difficulties which seem to confront me in whichever direction we go.

Assuming that the United States Congress, believing that the will of the people demands the policy of dissolution to be carried out, and assuming that it is car-ried out, in your opinion would that have an effect in the direction of lowering the prices of steel products to the consumer?

MR. CARNEGIE. Certainly it would, but—

MR. GARDNER. It would or it would not.

MR. CARNEGIE. It would lower the price.

MR. GARDNER. That is, dissolution would lower the price?

MR. CARNEGIE. Dissolution? No. I thought you said "the commission" instead of "dissolution." I thought you said the commission.

MR. GARDNER. No. I say, suppose that we take the course toward dissolution.

MR. CARNEGIE. Oh! I thought you said toward a commission.

MR. GARDNER. Would dissolution by the order of the courts of these large industrial units, in your opinion, result in lower prices to the consumer?

MR. CARNEGIE. It would depend upon what the court fixed.

MR. REED. You do not hear his question, Mr. Carnegie.

MR. CARNEGIE. I assume there would be—

MR. GARDNER. Just follow me a moment, Mr. Carnegie. I think it is very important to get your opinion on it. I say, supposing Congress rejects your idea of that commission?

MR. CARNEGIE. Yes.

MR. GARDNER. And takes the other course in deference to what they believe to be the will of the people and perhaps in accordance with their own judgment; and supposing these great units are dissolved by order of the court. In your opinion would that result in lower prices on steel products?

MR. CARNEGIE. Not unless there was a tribunal to fix prices. You mean that they can do anything of that sort and there would be destructive competition?

MR. GARDNER. We will say, instead of being the mere dissolution of the United States Steel Corporation and the resolution of all these constituent companies into independent companies, that it is even more drastic than that. Let it be as drastic as you choose. Would that, in your opinion, tend to lower prices for steel products?

MR. CARNEGIE. If there was a law by which they could not confer or unite in any way to make a common price?

MR. GARDNER. If you destroy them as they stand by dissolution and under the order of the court and do not establish the commission which you advocate and which I will admit is at all events worthy of consideration.

MR. CARNEGIE. Why, my dear sir, if you dissolve them into small parts they will do as they did before when they were small parts.

MR. GARDNER. Of course they will. Will that, in the long run, make cheaper steel products or more expensive steel products?

MR. CARNEGIE. No; because they would have understandings. They would be driven to understandings against destructive competition which would ruin them all.

MR. GARDNER. No matter what they are driven to, would it, in your opinion, result in the consumers of this country getting their steel cheaper in the long run?

MR. CARNEGIE. Not permanently; no, sir.

MR. GARDNER. That is your opinion?

MR. CARNEGIE. It is my opinion.

MR. GARDNER. That is one of the objections that is working in my mind to this dissolution process.

Let me go in the other direction and show you what is working in my mind

as an objection to your commission, which you propose.

Would you clothe this commission with the power to prescribe a maximum price for products which enter into interstate commerce?

MR. CARNEGIE. All products?

MR. GARDNER. All products.

MR. CARNEGIE. We are dealing now with steel, are we not — all products of steel?

MR. GARDNER. If you establish a court you must establish it under general laws.

MR. CARNEGIE. All manufactures?

MR. GARDNER. Yes. Then you would say that it should apply to all manufactures?

MR. CARNEGIE. Yes; certainly.

MR. GARDNER. That would allow them putting a price on any manufactured goods, irrespective of whether they were manufactured under a patent or no matter how competitive the business was.

Supposing it was some manufactures like the boot and shoe industry in my own districts, where each man is fighting every other man and where there is unlimited competition; would you say it was proper for the Government to have the right to set the price at which those articles should be sold?

MR. CARNEGIE. The maximum price?

MR. GARDNER. Yes.

MR. CARNEGIE. If it became necessary, I would.

MR. GARDNER. You would clothe them with that power, in case of necessity?

MR. CARNEGIE. Yes; that court to be the supreme judge.

MR. GARDNER. Suppose the whole people should enter into an agreement to take the maximum price, and everyone of them charge the maximum price, and that under ordinary forms of competition there would be many shoes sold under the maximum price; how would you reach a condition like that?

MR. CARNEGIE. I should not want to reach it.

MR. GARDNER. That is, you would permit the agreement that they should all charge the maximum price?

MR. CARNEGIE. Yes.

MR. GARDNER. I have indicated two of the difficulties which must work in any man's mind who is trying to systematize this thing, because it seems to me that the course of dissolution and the course of Government control are leading in two absolutely different directions, no matter how much we may confuse the issue today, and whether a man says he is for more drastic laws or for the amendment of the Sherman Act, when he means the repeal of the Sherman Act under an amendment form; that really the issue which is arising in men's minds is whether we shall follow a policy which, ultimately, leads to dissolution, or whether we shall follow a policy which ultimately leads to the recognition of the large units, coupled with absolute Government control, such as we have over the railroads.

MR. CARNEGIE. I think, sir, you and I differ in this: I see one next step clearly before me. I go there, and I leave my successors to manage affairs after I am gone. They will see the subject more clearly than you can imagine it or I can imagine it, and therefore I would take this indispensable step at the time.

* * *

Hearings before the Committee on
Interstate Commerce, U. S. Senate,
62 CONGRESS, 1 SESSION (1911)

A. *Testimony of George W. Perkins, Partner, J. P. Morgan Company, Director, International Harvester and United States Steel*

* * *

THE CHAIRMAN. Were you engaged in business when the Sherman antitrust law was passed?

MR. PERKINS. Not in mercantile business; no, sir.

THE CHAIRMAN. That law was passed at the time of comparative quiet, was it not?

MR. PERKINS. I would hardly say that. I would think it was passed, as we look back on it, at a time when these forces of which I speak, that have done so much to centralize business, were beginning to show their power.

THE CHAIRMAN. Yes; otherwise attention probably would not have been called to it. But you could hardly say that the Sherman antitrust law was passed in a period of excitement or hysteria; in other words, that it was calmly and carefully considered?

MR. PERKINS. I am not in position to say as to that, but I do feel this, that at that very time when the Sherman law was passed, sufficient thought and study was not given to the causes that were at work, and that were destined to revolutionize business methods.

THE CHAIRMAN. Do you believe, Mr. Perkins, that any amount of deliberation can frame the details of a plan for regulating forces where the conditions under which those forces exist are constantly changing, developing, and progressing?

MR. PERKINS. I do not believe that the world will, in any respect, be a finished product for a very long time. I think each generation should do in its time what it can to improve conditions, not in a selfish way, but with a view to making them better and more stable, having very careful regard not to lay down any practice that would be detrimental to the oncoming generations.

THE CHAIRMAN. That is true, but you spoke of a period of investigation and the process of investigation and temporary relief prior to the adoption of a permanent plan. Now, can any system be adopted in a growing country except the system of what is best and wisest, for the time being, in anticipation of change?

MR. PERKINS. This memorandum that I have read to you is meant to express just exactly what it states, of course. My own belief is that we have got to come to national incorporation of large interstate business enterprises. Whether you gentlemen are willing to admit that and enact it now, I do not know. I have taken it for granted that perhaps that could not be done this winter, but to immediately expand the Bureau of Corporations by giving it power enough to license these large combinations, occurred to me might be feasible and might not be a very long step in advance, but was along the line that we have used in other business enterprises, and certainly, Mr. Chairman, immediate relief is most

desirable — I mean relief from the uncertainty in which every business man who is doing anything that approaches a large business finds himself.

THE CHAIRMAN. Well, does that really apply to the man who is approaching a large business simply because it is a large business, or apply to the phase, rather, of the proposed activities of the business without so much reference to its size?

MR. PERKINS. Does anybody know that? Where can anybody go to find that out?

THE CHAIRMAN. If to-day you wanted to start a boot and shoe factory, is there anything in this situation which would embarrass you in the contemplation of the amount of capital you could put into that business?

MR. PERKINS. Well, I think there are two answers to that. First, yes; I think there is.

THE CHAIRMAN. What?

MR. PERKINS. The amount of percentage of the business that the man might be doing if he put in more than a certain amount of capital.

THE CHAIRMAN. Suppose you contemplated to-day starting a boot and shoe factory, is there anything in the present situation with reference to the Sherman antitrust law that would embarrass you the slightest in the question of whether you might invest a million or $100,000,000 in that factory?

MR. PERKINS. You are speaking now of starting an entirely new business?

THE CHAIRMAN. Exactly.

MR. PERKINS. No; probably not. If the business developed until it reached a point where the man might be in doubt as to what percentage of the total business he was doing. By that time he would have had a very large number of small stockholders, all over the world. Then somebody would swoop down on

him and say, "Here, you are doing too
much of this business," or, "You are not
doing the business along proper lines."
And then these small stockholders would
suffer.

THE CHAIRMAN. Yes; but you suggest
two alternatives. One is the suggestion,
"You are doing too much business," or
the other, "You are not doing it along
proper lines." Now I eliminate the
proper lines for the moment and confine my inquiry to the extent of the business. Is there anything to-day in the
Sherman antitrust law, in its relation to
the present attitude of the Government,
which would embarrass you at any point
in the mere question of how much capital you could put into this factory in its
operation?

MR. PERKINS. I think there is.

THE CHAIRMAN. Please state what it is.

MR. PERKINS. I think it embarrasses
business at what you might call the twilight zone; that is, the man does not
know how far he can go, and that is particularly true of any company that gets
to be large enough, where it is out for
foreign trade, and at the same time doing
a domestic business.

THE CHAIRMAN. Has the suggestion
ever been made that the mere question
of the amount of capital employed in a
business — independent now of the manner of conducting that business with
reference to controlling a number of
subordinate enterprises — has presented
itself as in possible conflict with the
Sherman antitrust law?

MR. PERKINS. I would answer that no,
as to any decisions that have been rendered; but yes, as to about eight-tenths
of the manner in which the case has been
presented to the people.

THE CHAIRMAN. Yes, but in every case,
Mr. Perkins, the paramount and basic
cause of complaint has been the manner

of conducting the business, its bearing
upon the question of restraint of trade
or monopoly, and the size of the business a mere incident, as proof bearing
upon the ultimate question of its either
being in restraint of trade or a monopoly.
Is not that so?

MR. PERKINS. I think that is regarded
as the legal question, but there are a
number of great moral questions in this
that I believe the people, if you could
line them up man by man, are more
deeply concerned with than they are with
the legal end of it. May I illustrate that?

THE CHAIRMAN. I expect to get to that
in a moment —

MR. PERKINS. Excuse me for interrupt-
ing you. Let me use this illustration that
just comes to my mind. We have had a
good many important lawsuits under the
Sherman Act of late and some decisions.
Within a week after the last suit had
been filed, namely, the steel suit, an interest in New York announced that it was
going to organize a company by putting
600 stores together, as an operating company, and that those stores were to be
all over the United States, and some
abroad. They were going to organize that
company with $16,000,000 of preferred
and $50,000,000 of common stock. Now
of course that was being done to expand
their business and they were going to
get that money from the public. Everybody knew right off that that was not
a business that was going to be done
by one State or with stockholders in a
neighborhood, or with customers in a
neighborhood.

Now, there is a great moral question
involved there. That money was to be
gathered in from a large number of small
stockholders and then the company
would go on and do business. It would
get its charter from the State, but it was
doing business all over the world. I be-

lieve — and I am very firm in my belief — that one of the things that the people of this country are deeply concerned about is how a company like that is going to be capitalized to begin with, and how it is going to conduct its business from the moral point of view after it starts, and that men who undertake as large a business as that, restraint or no restraint of trade, themselves really want to be checked up by some authority, as big as they are, that will say to the public and those investors, "This is fair business and is being conducted properly."

Now, there is nothing under the Sherman law that provides that; and, after all, the people go back to the morals of the case.

THE CHAIRMAN. Yes; I wish they would.

MR. PERKINS. They do; they are all right.

THE CHAIRMAN. We did not hear very much of this phase of discussion, however, until the Government began to interfere with these so-called combinations.

MR. PERKINS. Well, Mr. Chairman, I think that business men in this country have been so engrossed in the possibilities of developing trade, the growth of intercommunication has been so colossal, their opportunities have been so enormous, their noses have been so much to the grindstone, that they overlook very largely, if you please, their responsibility to the public on this question.

THE CHAIRMAN. I quite agree with you.

MR. PERKINS. And I think you must not lose sight — and it is extremely important not to lose sight — of the fact that there has been a great awakening in the last four or five years on this moral question, and that business generally is being conducted with far greater regard to those questions than it was five years

ago. We have made splendid progress along those lines.

THE CHAIRMAN. Now, coming back to this boot and shoe industry that I want to establish, you start in with that, we will say, with a million dollars of capital. You do a very small percentage of business at first. Now, assuming that all the growth of that business is independent of any reprehensible methods or methods subject to criticism — you expand the business until you make 75 per cent of the boots and shoes of this country. Now, is there anything in the Sherman anti-trust law or in the attitude of the Government — mark you, independent of the method of your business — which would embarrass you in the development of that business upon the sole basis that you were making 75 per cent of the boots and shoes of this country?

MR. PERKINS. Well, Mr. Chairman, I do not know; but if you are correct, then I can not for the life of me see the difference between obtaining 75 per cent of the business that way and obtaining 75 per cent of the business by consolidating, because when you once have it you have the potential power.

THE CHAIRMAN. That may be; but I am dealing now with the Sherman anti-trust law and the attitude of the Government in relation to it. Now, Mr. Perkins, is there any line of production in this country where there is a demand for the product for which it is impossible to get capital to supply that demand, assuming that the demand is fairly recognized as a business proposition?

MR. PERKINS. That would be a very difficult question to answer. I am not in touch with all branches of trade; but speaking broadly, I think there is no doubt but that at the moment capital is extremely timid about undertaking new enterprises.

THE CHAIRMAN. I am assuming now that it is plain as a business proposition that the demand exists. If we could assume that we needed twice as many wagons in this country as we have to-day, do you think there would be any difficulty in getting capital to build those wagons because of anything in the Sherman antitrust law?

MR. PERKINS. I do not think that is quite the point at which business —

THE CHAIRMAN. But that is the question I am asking, however.

MR. PERKINS. Well, you could take one particular line; for instance, wagons, where of course it is a simple question and can easily dispose of that, but the principle of developing American business is very different, and there is nothing that is so timid as domestic capital, unless it be foreign capital.

THE CHAIRMAN. That is true, but I press the question again. Assuming that it could be met by asserting that there would be a sale for twice as many wagons as we are making to-day at a fair price, and that would return a good profit, would there be any difficulty about getting the wagons made?

MR. PERKINS. I do not think there would, as to wagons.

* * *

THE CHAIRMAN. Perhaps not. Is there anything in the Sherman antitrust law, or the attitude of the Government in relation to it, that would embarrass any business concern in contemplating the efficiency or increased efficiency of its business?

MR. PERKINS. Yes, sir; I think there is.

THE CHAIRMAN. What is it? We will now take this boot and shoe factory that we have got started. You contemplate some increased efficiency, the application of better machines or any other way

you may suggest yourself. Now, what is there in the Sherman antitrust law, or the attitudes of the Government in relation to it, that would interfere with that?

MR. PERKINS. The principal thing that would interfere with it, as I understand it — and I admit that I am not a lawyer and am not qualified to speak by the card of the Sherman law — but as I understand it, the objection would be the point to which that company could have a business relation and understanding with its competitors.

THE CHAIRMAN. Oh, yes. Then, in other words, the only embarrassment that confronts contemplated enterprises, or the extension of present enterprises, is that embarrassment which grows out of the method of the business with relation to competition.

MR. PERKINS. No; I would not say it was the only one.

THE CHAIRMAN. Well, what other one is there?

MR. PERKINS. The one I cited here a while ago, where you said that if a company were to start in a modest way and actually grew to the point of having 75 per cent of the business.

THE CHAIRMAN. Why, Mr. Perkins, do you seriously contend that there is a suggestion in the antitrust law, or in the attitude of the Government, that there would come a time of embarrassment in the running of this boot and shoe factory based upon the sole question of the percentage of the product which is produced in this country?

MR. PERKINS. I do not know. I would like to have somebody tell me, but I will answer it in another way. Do you think we have reached a point in this country where the people, without regulation, without any hand being on such a concern, would be willing that a given concern should produce 75 or 85 per cent of the boots and shoes, and one set of men would have the power to do that?

THE CHAIRMAN. I do not think the people would object to that unless it involved an objection to the method and practice they employed in their business.

MR. PERKINS. Who would say as to what their method of objection would be?

THE CHAIRMAN. Primarily Congress, of course.

MR. PERKINS. Then we come to regulations, where we meet. I agree with you.

THE CHAIRMAN. You are getting on to method. I am dealing not with method but the mere growth of business.

MR. PERKINS. I do not think you can separate them, Mr. Chairman. I do not think it is really possible.

* * *

SENATOR CUMMINS. You have said you were not a lawyer, you have no professional training, and therefore I will not try to examine with regard to the technical features of the antitrust law. But as you know the two effective sections of the antitrust law are the first and second; the one prohibiting agreements and combinations and conspiracies in restraint of trade, and the other prohibiting monopoly or the attempt to create monopolies?

MR. PERKINS. Yes, sir.

SENATOR CUMMINS. Now, inasmuch as the antitrust law, which I have just summarized, is the only thing, from your standpoint, which has brought uncertainty or difficulty in the business world, that can be changed or removed, I wish you would tell the committee, what, in your judgment, business men ought to be permitted to do which is prohibited by this law, and known to be prohibited by the law or what business men want to do which may be in doubt under this law.

Our purpose is to find out whether this law needs any amendment, supplement, or change in order to serve the welfare of the people. Now, in order to do that we want to know from men of your experience what it is that business enterprises desire to do which they are now prohibited from doing, or what they want to do concerning which there is somewhat doubt and that they are unwilling to do?

MR. PERKINS. I think it is at least as important to find out what ought to be done for the benefit of our people, and then business ought to be reorganized to accomplish that. The rapid changes that have taken place in methods — and I believe are going to be just as rapid the next 25 years — make me feel that you can not lay down many very specific rules, but that we have got to have here in Washington a controlling commission, composed largely of business men, to which a business enterprise could come and say, "Now we want to thus and so; here is our capitalization; here are the methods we are going to employ; here is the manner in which we propose to treat labor; here is the manner in which we are going to treat our competitors, and here is the method of treating our consumers. Is this in keeping with good public policy?" And find out whether or not they can do it.

Now of course I realize the great difficulty that you gentlemen are going to meet is, what is the specific thing, and in doing that you perhaps address your thoughts to banks and railroads and other things where regulations have been made.

Business is very different. There are hardly any two lines of business, as we know, that are alike, and you can not lay down a hard and fast rule that will cover them. For instance, I cited the telephone business; 80 or 90 per cent of the telephone business may be considered desirable. You may not want to put 80 or 90 per cent of the steel business in commerce; in some other business 50 per cent might be a potential factor in the method employed by one business, and you may not want to employ it in another. It is going to be an exceedingly difficult and delicate thing to adjust, and I do not believe you can do very much at it with specific rules. I think you have got to give to a controlling commission very broad power that in practical business questions would be analogous to the power, so to speak, of the Supreme Court; that when this commission would say so and so is in the public interest, or it is not, that the country would accept that. I do not say that that would be our permanent policy for a century, but as it stands now, in our relationship to Germany and other countries, we have got to take some such step as the first step and then watch it and round it out as evolution goes on.

SENATOR CUMMINS. I did not intend to call so much for the methods as for your opinion with regard to what the law should set up as a standard for any commission or any board that might be organized to administer the law. We have the antitrust law. Now do you know of anything that business men, whether in large affairs or small affairs, have wanted to do for the betterment of their business which the antitrust law prohibits?

MR. PERKINS. Well, I may say that there is the twilight zone; there is the doubt.

SENATOR CUMMINS. But there is an illuminated zone under the law as well as a twilight zone, I am sure. There are some things which everybody now agrees are prohibited by the law.

MR. PERKINS. That is right.

SENATOR CUMMINS. Now, which are of those things, or what of those things, do business men think they ought to be permitted to do?

MR. PERKINS. What is restraint of trade and what is restraint of competition? I, for instance, feel that we certainly do not want restraint of trade — and by restraint of trade I mean curtailment and unnatural contraction of trade — but I can easily understand, from my practical experience in the world, how a certain proper restraint of competition might mean expanding trade. Now, I do not believe that we ought to have to go through a lawsuit and through the courts to determine that. It is essentially a practical question.

SENATOR CUMMINS. There is very much force in that, but in order to adjust the law to meet these necessities we must have a comprehension of what kind of things the business world wants to do that it can not now do, and which it knows it can not do. I will make it a little more concrete. There have been many — at least some — very prominent men before us who believe, and have expressed their belief to us, that business concerns engaged in a common business, the same kind of business, ought to be permitted to come together, and, in order to protect themselves against what is called ruinous competition, enter into agreement that would fix the price at which their commodities should be sold. Everybody knows that that is prohibited by the antitrust law. Now, do you believe that the law ought to be so changed, no matter whether it is administered by the courts or administered by a board, to permit agreements of that kind?

MR. PERKINS. I do not think that we have reached a point in our evolution where we should attempt fixing prices.

I think that would be going out into a realm of affairs that would be almost endless. But there might be a business, almost any time, developed to a point where a certain restraint on prices by such a commission as I have named would be desirable.

SENATOR CUMMINS. Well, do you mean a restraint upon high prices or upon low prices?

MR. PERKINS. Restraint rather more in the nature of a maximum price. But the reverse of that would be true, if a concern was using its power to fix a low price in a given community.

SENATOR CUMMINS. What the business world, I take it, is really afraid of is that through the operation of the antitrust law the country will be restored to what has been termed here "old-fashioned competition."

MR. PERKINS. Yes; that is one thing.

SENATOR CUMMINS. And that thereby the profits of business will be impaired or destroyed. Is that your view of the real difficulty?

MR. PERKINS. I think it is more than that, Senator Cummins. I think that any one of us around this table can remember when in almost every line of business we were having very extreme fluctuations in prices, resulting every once in awhile in industrial panic and prostration, with certain failures in this or in the other line

of business, and the throwing of labor out of employment, and a very unhappy time, which came about largely through competition of that kind which was either reckless in its overproduction, bringing this about, or reckless in many other ways brought about by bad management.

SENATOR CUMMINS. How would you propose to prevent that kind of competition?

MR. PERKINS. I do not think you can do it by an act that you will draw that is specific, because I think the changing conditions are so rapid, in the first place, and the changed conditions of one business compared to another are so different, that you can not put it in a statute.

For instance, I noticed the other day in reading an account of how the Sherman Act was drawn at first, that there was one time in the history of its discussion when a large number of things were thought to be desirable to put in the act which were not put in the act in the end, and they reached the point where they had to boil them down to where the act is now. It seems to me we are in that situation now; that the question of what can be done with each specific business has got to be largely left to the integrity of the man on a commission whom the countries will more or less trust, at least as a beginning. We will learn pretty soon what we can do.

B. Testimony of Louis D. Brandeis, Lawyer and Reformer

SENATOR CUMMINS. Mr. Brandeis, you are a lawyer by profession?

MR. BRANDEIS. Yes, sir.

SENATOR CUMMINS. And you are familiar with the decisions of the Supreme Court construing, interpreting, and applying the antitrust law, I take it?

MR. BRANDEIS. I have read them.

SENATOR CUMMINS. Do you recognize

that under those decisions there may be a monopoly in violation of the second section of the act that does not embrace or include all the field in which it operates?

MR. BRANDEIS. I think so.

SENATOR CUMMINS. We are coming gradually to understand that a monopoly is a concern or industrial financial institution that has the power to drive substantial competition out of the region in which it works. That is our idea now of monopoly, is it not?

MR. BRANDEIS. I think so.

SENATOR CUMMINS. And whenever a corporation grows large enough to be able to dominate and control the field, then it is exercising, or may exercise, a monopolistic power even though there still remain in the field concerns or establishments that are known as competitive?

MR. BRANDEIS. Certainly.

SENATOR CUMMINS. Do you believe that a corporation can be so offensive to the antitrust law on account of its size, even though it does not employ any of the vicious or unjust practices that have been characteristic of some of the trusts of which you have spoken?

MR. BRANDEIS. I should think it certainly might if it originated in combination.

SENATOR CUMMINS. Ought there not, therefore, to be some instrumentality of the law that would determine how large a corporation should become or be, even before it may be finally condemned through a prosecution against it under the antitrust law?

MR. BRANDEIS. I am inclined to think yes. Perhaps if I might —

SENATOR CUMMINS. Do not confine yourself to categorical answers, but give us your views upon the subject that may be contained in the question.

MR. BRANDEIS. I thank you. I have had no belief that up to the present time a question had arisen in regard to any corporation in that narrow form in which you put it; that is, each one of the large corporations I have had to deal with have been objectionable on grounds other than size merely. I have considered and do consider that the proposition that mere bigness can not be an offense against society is false, because I believe that our society, which rests upon democracy, can not endure under such conditions. Something approaching equality is essential. You may have an organization in the community which is so powerful that in a particular branch of the trade it may dominate by mere size. Although its individual practices may be according to rules, it may be, nevertheless, a menace to the community; and I may add further that, in my opinion, it was bad legislation which removed all limits to the size of corporations, as we did from 10 to 20 years ago.

SENATOR CUMMINS. I will take up the concrete example that you have mentioned, and a great many others are mentioned here — the United States Steel Corporation. Suppose that we had had in 1901 a board such as has been described by various witnesses here and intended in a sense to apply the antitrust law to actual affairs, and you had been a member of that board and the proposers or promoters of this enterprise had come to the board saying that they were about to organize a corporation that would take unto itself a little more than 60 per cent of the whole business in which they were to engage. Now, apart from the vice of its capitalization, which everybody recognizes I think, would you have been in favor of permitting such a corporation to organize, receive a license under the Federal law, and to engage in interstate commerce, and if you would not have been in favor of it, give us the reasons which would have governed you.

MR. BRANDEIS. If, as a member of that commission, I had had the legal power to deny them the right to incorporate, I should have certainly refused them that right. I should have done it because I believe that the creation of such a large unit was necessarily an evil influence in the community. In the first place, I should have been convinced that that amount of capital was not necessary for the creation of the most efficient instrument of production and distribution that could have been created, and in the second place, even if it should have been true that as a mere engine of production and distribution this unit would have been more efficient than a smaller one, I should have been convinced that the inherent, the incidental, social, and political ills which would attend the creation of that huge power would bring about evils to the community which would many times outweigh the advantage, the slight advantage, if any, which would come from an increased efficiency.

Now take, for instance, this incidental situation. We had last year in the Advanced Rate case, when the railroads of this country were clamoring for an increase in rates because there had been granted increases in wages — we had this situation. I asked the presidents — President McRae, of the Pennsylvania, and President Brown, of the New York Central — specifically, whether, when they got together to consider ways and means of increasing their revenues, they had made any effort to secure a reduction in the cost of steel rails. It was perfectly obvious, according to their own argument, that at lessened prices larger purchases would have been not only helpful to them but helpful to the whole industry of the country, and advance it in different ways — "Did you undertake in any way to secure a reduction in the price of steel rails?" And they both said "No."

Now, what was the situation? It was that the directors of the United States Steel Corporation were directors in most of the large railroad systems of this country. The railroads were directly or indirectly controlled in a certain way by the same men who were the directors of the Steel Corporation. Now, that is one of the powers; that is one of the incidents of this big business. I say that we have got to start at the very beginning with this inquiry, that if we create a huge financial industrial entity, are not the dangers so great that even if they were of an advantage we risk our whole system, judicial, political, and industrial, by creating a power which we can not control, as happened when the United States Steel Corporation was formed 10 years ago?

SENATOR CUMMINS. I take it for granted that you believe in corporations of sufficient size to employ all reasonable advantages looking toward the reduction in cost of production?

MR. BRANDEIS. Certainly.

SENATOR CUMMINS. It has been assumed here constantly by a great many people who appeared before us that the larger a corporation becomes the less will the cost of production be. You have already addressed yourself somewhat to that subject, but I want you to be a little more definite upon this. There are some things that can be done by large concerns to reduce the cost of production that ought not to be done looking to the welfare of society, I take it.

MR. BRANDEIS. Yes; and I am very glad that your suggestion enables me to say what I believe the function of the Government in this respect to be. I said this morning that in order to preserve competition the Government should provide for certain regulation of competition in order to prevent excesses which lead to monopoly. The Government has besides important affirmative duties in respect to aiding competition; a large part of our advance in agriculture during the last 10 years (and advance will come I am sure with accelerated speed during the next 10 years) is due to the Government's agricultural experiment stations. We have applied the collective ability and resources of America to teach the farmer how to make profitable the work he was doing. That is a very proper function of the Government. It was important that that should be done by the Government, so that every farmer in the United States, present or prospective, might have the benefit of those researches and that instruction.

Now, in industry a similar step ought to be taken. It ought not to happen that the United States Steel Corporation, by reason merely of its ability to spend large amounts on laboratories and research, should far outstrip its competitors. If an advance in industry is to be made as a result of expensive research which is not immediately remunerative, the Government ought to undertake the investigation, so that everybody who wishes to engage in the industry could have the benefit of the knowledge acquired, just as we give our citizens opportunities for education in many other ways, just as we give to the merchants the results of expensive consular inquiries, and just as we are distributing other information through the Department of Commerce and Labor. Whenever industry requires for its advance investigations of that character which are so expensive that only a huge concern can assume the burden, then it is the Government's function to secure the information for all the people. Such a bureau of industrial research would be a great aid to competition. Furthermore, it would open up fields of advance in industry which have been closed hitherto even in times of unrestricted competition.

For there are now all over this country people who are fertile of ideas who are as eager to advance industry as the scientists are in other spheres of activity. They know now that if they invent there is little chance of finding anybody to develop their inventions. I can speak on this subject from experience.

After I suggested last year in the advanced rate hearings that there were many methods of improving the efficiency of the railroads which had not been adopted I received floods of letters from all parts of the country, from men here, there, and everywhere, who thought they had valuable inventions or ideas leading to economies. Many of these ideas were, according to such advice as I could get, very meritorious. But in the absence of a Government bureau to sift them and make known the valuable ones they will doubtless die unused.

There ought to be a Government bureau or experiment station which would sift the presumably valuable from the valueless and which could hold out to the American people — filled as they are with ideas and with the desire to advance the processes of industry — the certainty that if they could contribute matters of value they would receive due recognition. We should then reap in the field of industry the same profitable results which are already coming from our agricultural experiment stations.

SENATOR CUMMINS. Mr. Brandeis, from your observation and experience, both of which have been great, do you know of any legitimate process or advantage in reducing cost in the steel business that can be employed by the United States Steel Corporation that could not as successfully be employed by a corporation of $100,000,000 of capital?

MR. BRANDEIS. I do not, and I do not believe that there is any.

SENATOR CUMMINS. And if, in 1901, we had had some governmental function that would have restricted the capital that any corporation engaged in it should use to $100,000,000 or $200,000,000, we would have had a good many corporations engaged in the business doing it upon substantially even terms, not only as to the direct process of manufacture of product, but even terms in the business world, would we not, necessarily?

MR. BRANDEIS. We should, if we had also buttressed that law so as to prevent common ownership of stock in the several corporations.

SENATOR CUMMINS. Precisely; I was just coming to that. Healthful and reasonable and effective competition is hardly to be looked for so long as there is a community of interest in socalled competing corporations, I suppose.

MR. BRANDEIS. I so believe.

SENATOR CUMMINS. That seems to be a deduction from what we know of human nature, and therefore if we could provide that these great concerns should not have common stockholders we would make a very considerable advance toward reasonable competition, I assume.

MR. BRANDEIS. I think so; but I think that the question of the limitation of the size of the corporation, if we had an effective law regulating trusts, would not become an urgent question very soon, although it may be a simple way of arriving at the result. To express a little more clearly what I mean, I will say this: I believe that the existing trusts have acquired the position which they hold largely through methods which are in and of themselves reprehensible. I mean either through methods which are abuses of competition or by such methods as were pursued by the steel corporation in paying ridiculous values for property for the purpose of monopolistic control.

I am so firmly convinced that the large unit is not as efficient — I mean the very large unit — is not as efficient as the

smaller unit, that I believe if it were possible to-day to make the corporations act in accordance with what doubtless all of us would agree should be the rules of trade no huge corporation would be created, or, if created, would be successful. I do not mean by that to say that it is not good to have the limitation in the law. What I mean is that I am so convinced of the economic fallacy in the huge unit that if we make competition possible, if we create conditions where there could be reasonable competition, that these monsters would fall to the ground, that I do not consider the need of such a limitation urgent.

SENATOR CUMMINS. By that you mean, I take it, at least partially, that if we had some regulation which would insure honest capitalization — that is, bonds and stocks, that measure of actual value of the property taken in by the corporation — there would be a greatly less motive for bringing them together?

MR. BRANDEIS. I mean that; but I mean something more, and it is this: Go back and see what the real commanding cause was of the formation of these trusts. In the first place, I do not believe the desire for greater efficiency was an important moving cause. The potent causes were two things — one was to avoid what those interested deemed destructive or, at least, very annoying competition; the other cause, an extremely effective cause, was the desire of promoters and bankers for huge commissions. The amount of Steel Trust representing bankers' commissions was figured by the Commissioner of Corporations as $150,000,000 in securities.

SENATOR POMERENE. Commissions?

MR. BRANDEIS. The commission was $150,000,000, as they figured it out. I mean commissions or the syndicate's charges on $1,402,000,000 of securities issued and issue of other companies controlled by the trust. Of course, the desire for commissions and promoters' profits was a potent cause. Then there was the desire to capitalize failures; that is, as many steel men saw that as against Carnegie competition would be ineffective, they desired to capitalize their inability to compete with Mr. Carnegie. As a necessary incident of that they had to get Carnegie out of the way, and, as Mr. Perkins indicated, they were, to accomplish this, ready to pay Mr. Carnegie not merely the value of his business, measured on any proper basis, but the value of the ability of Mr. Carnegie to do them harm. This was capitalized, and consequently they paid to Mr. Carnegie many times the real value of his business.

Now that paying many times the real value for that business was practically bribing Mr. Carnegie to go out of business, the bribe being paid by the American people; but it was a bribing of Mr. Carnegie to go out of that business in order that these less efficient businesses might not be destroyed. Instead, therefore — and that is an operation which the Commissioner of Corporations sets forth very clearly in his report — instead of that operation being in aid of efficiency its result was to destroy efficiency, because all of these corporations were doing business on an efficiency basis far below that which Mr. Carnegie had attained.

* * *

SENATOR CUMMINS. What regulations that will restrict competition within reasonable limits do you suggest?

MR. BRANDEIS. I think this might be a very brief statement of some of the practices which ought to be deemed in and of themselves unreasonable, and therefore illegal, if connected with the restraint of trade: Selling in one locality at discriminating prices in order to force out local competition; selling one grade or variety at discriminating prices to force out competition; discriminating against producers who will not agree not to deal with a rival; imposing terms in leases that the lessees shall not buy or lease anything from anyone else; spying on competitors; bribing methods; buying trade secrets; establishing bogus competition.

I think practices of that nature, which are all what might be called methods of destruction, and are not properly called competition at all, ought to be made impossible.

SENATOR CUMMINS. We have acquired the term "in restraint of trade," which we have been told many times, both here and from the decisions of the Supreme Court, is based upon the common law. Of course you recognize that some of those things were not known in the common law as restraint of trade. Now, your idea is that we ought to, say, enlarge upon the common law so as to make these things which experience has shown are opposed to the public welfare restraint of trade, and thereby bring them within the prohibition of the antitrust law.

MR. BRANDEIS. Yes; if it is necessary to do that. That is, I have no hesitation in saying that those practices are not proper practices for business; and it is clear to me that if they are exercised in connection with any restraint of trade they ought to be conclusively accepted as evidence of illegality or unreasonableness, as the court expresses it.

SENATOR CUMMINS. There are some of us who hesitate — and I am one — to accept the idea that there can be any reasonable restraint of trade. I can easily imagine a restraint upon competition that is not a restraint upon trade; but if the given thing is in restraint of trade, which means of course that freedom of commerce which is necessary for the public good, then it ought to be illegal, and I take it that your general notion is that, viewed from the standpoint of our experience in modern times, we ought to make the words "restraint of trade" mean what the people of this country believe they ought to mean in order to accomplish their own welfare.

MR. BRANDEIS. That is my belief, decidedly.

SENATOR CUMMINS. I think that is all.

SENATOR NEWLANDS. Mr. Brandeis, what limit would you place upon the size of corporations?

MR. BRANDEIS. I should not think that we are in a position today to fix a limit, stated in millions of dollars, but I think we are in a position, after the experience of the last 20 years, to state two things: In the first place, that a corporation may well be too large to be the most efficient instrument of production and of distribution, and, in the second place, whether it has exceeded the point of greatest economic efficiency or not, it may be too large to be tolerated among the people who desire to be free. I think, therefore, that the recognition of those propositions should underlie any administration of the law. As I stated before, I believe that it was a very serious mistake on the part of our legislators to remove the limit of the assets and of capitalization of corporations; that they did not fully consider what they were doing. I believe it is historically true that that limit was removed without serious consideration by the legislators of the country of the probable effect of their action.

SENATOR NEWLANDS. Do you think it would be in the power of the United States Government, by act of Congress,

to limit the size of State corporations engaged in interstate commerce, either in point of size, capitalization, or area of their operations?

MR. BRANDEIS. I do not suppose it would be constitutional in one sense to limit their size, but I suppose Congress would possess the constitutional power to confine the privilege of interstate commerce to corporations of a particular character.

SENATOR NEWLANDS. You have no question about that power?

MR. BRANDEIS. I should think not.

SENATOR NEWLANDS. It would be necessary to fix some standard, would it not?

MR. BRANDEIS. I think so; yes, sir.

SENATOR NEWLANDS. Upon which or by which the administrative bureau or commission charged with the duty could determine whether the corporation was of a size that threatened to become a monopoly or that threatened, as you say, social efficiency. Now, what standard would you fix; how would you phrase it?

MR. BRANDEIS. I do not think that I am able at this time to state the exact provision which I should make. I feel very clear on the proposition, but I do not feel equally clear as to what machinery should be invoked or the specific provision by which that proposition could be enforced.

SENATOR NEWLANDS. You do not think that standard should be fixed in dollars; you have already stated that.

MR. BRANDEIS. I am very clear that the maximum limit could not be properly fixed in dollars, because what would be just enough for one business would be far too much for many others.

SENATOR NEWLANDS. Then, if it is not fixed in dollars, would it not be necessary to fix it in respect to the area of the operations, the proportion of the business, or of the industry which the corporation would be likely to absorb?

MR. BRANDEIS. There is embodied some such suggestion in the La Follette bill. It seems to me that probably this goes rather to the volume of business than to capitalization, but the more I have thought of the subject in connection with the tobacco disintegration, in which case I acted as counsel and investigated trade facts, it seems to me that there is a distinct peril in the community in having one organization control a very large percentage of the market. The La Follette bill provides that where there is found to be a combination in restraint of trade, if the combination controls 40 per cent or more of the market, that creates a presumption of unreasonableness. I am inclined to think that an inquiry into our experience of the last 20 years would justify making of that presumption irrefutable, and that no corporation ought to control so large a percentage if we desire to maintain competition at all. I found, for instance, in the tobacco company this situation — and it was one of the many objections to the plan of so-called disintegration — that the American Tobacco Co. in various departments were controlling about 40 per cent or over of the American business. We found there that in this way the American Tobacco Co. alone, and each one of the other two large companies, would control a proportion of the total business of the country in certain departments of the trade which was from one to seven times the aggregate of the business of all of the independents. Now, I believe that fair competition is not possible under those conditions, because the mere power of endurance of the large company would be sufficient to give it mastery of the field.

SENATOR NEWLANDS. And yet, if you were establishing to-day a standard to which corporations hereafter organized, we will say, for the purpose of engaging in both interstate and State commerce, should conform, you would not permit any such corporation to control 40 per cent of the business, would you?

MR. BRANDEIS. I do not think I should. I mean the more I have thought of it the less inclined I have been to allow that.

SENATOR NEWLANDS. Would you be willing to allow one-tenth in a country as large as this?

MR. BRANDEIS. I am inclined to think it could control one-tenth with perfect safety.

SENATOR NEWLANDS. You would not go below that?

MR. BRANDEIS. I would not prohibit it, and I should be perfectly prepared to allow any appreciable larger percentage to be controlled by one company.

SENATOR NEWLANDS. You say you would be?

MR. BRANDEIS. I would be prepared to allow considerably more than one-tenth. The doubt I had was whether 40 was not too much, and I was going down from 40.

SENATOR NEWLANDS. Now, if you were to establish such a standard, would you apply it only to corporations hereafter organized or endeavor to apply it to corporations already organized?

MR. BRANDEIS. I should, in the first place, naturally apply it to those corporations already organized which had been organized in violation of the Sherman antitrust law. I think that is the real question which confronts the country, and it is one on which there ought not to be hesitation, because, as I indicated today in another connection, it seems to me that it goes to the very foundations of society. The things which have been done in defiance of law should not be ratified. The danger of so doing is infinitely greater to society than any danger from the fall of securities or questions of credit, or anything of that kind. As I view it, we are in a position that is serious because of the distrust of our laws, and of our courts and such an act as the validation of things illegal will be one of the most serious steps that could be taken. We have been confronted with that situation in Massachusetts. We validated on one occasion violations of the law by a great corporation which are comparable to the violation of the Sherman law, and I think the demoralizing effect upon the community has been great, the unrest in the community increased, and also the doubt whether the law is being applied equally to the rich and to the poor. I look with the greatest apprehension upon any action on the part of Congress that would seem to condone violations of the law, particularly those committed by the rich.

SENATOR NEWLANDS. You would apply, then, this standard as to the percentage of the business, or the proportion of the business, or the area of the operations, whatever it may be, of corporations, not only to corporations that are hereafter to be organized, but also to those now organized that have been condemned under the Sherman Act, and I presume you would extend it to those that may be organized hereafter.

MR. BRANDEIS. Yes; that should be those that have been guilty of violations of the law.

SENATOR NEWLANDS. Now, as applied to those great aggregations of capital that now exist, whose securities are now upon the market, and are in use as securities for bank loans, etc., what importance do you attach to a movement that would practically retire those securities and result in the issue of securities of a different character, perhaps very much less in amount — I am speaking now of the effect not so much upon the owners of securities but upon the general prosperity of the country itself?

MR. BRANDEIS. I believe it would have very slight effect upon the general prosperity of the country — I mean slight evil effects — and that it will have very great effect, ultimately beneficial effect, upon the prosperity of the country if the people should understand that the law will be enforced equally against the rich and the poor, or against the capitalist or the laborer.

SENATOR NEWLANDS. You would regard it as a wise thing to have a gradual process of adjustment, would you not, rather than an immediate one?

MR. BRANDEIS. I think certainly it is very desirable to have the community accustom itself to the idea of change before a change is made, but I think Mr. Perkins's statement yesterday in answer to a somewhat similar question put to him by you, that a large amount of money is borrowed on such collateral for commercial purposes, would be found to be entirely unfounded.

I do not believe people who are engaging in commercial business are to any large extent investing in Standard Oil and Tobacco and similar securities and then borrowing money on them for the benefit of their business. I happen to know, from investigations which have been made in connection with another trust — the Sugar Trust — that its securities are held in the main by a very different class of persons than business men. The women of New England seem to own the great bulk of the securities of the American Sugar Refining Co., and I think it will be found so with regard to a very large number of our other securities. Of course there are those who are speculating in securities.

SENATOR NEWLANDS. Your idea then is that they are held either for investment or speculation as a rule?

MR. BRANDEIS. To a very large extent — not exclusively.

SENATOR NEWLANDS. But the case you speak of in Massachusetts, where the stocks are held largely by women — who never do wrong, of course, and who must be innocent purchasers — what do you say regarding the effect upon them of a radical readjustment in these securities that would inflict a loss upon them?

MR. BRANDEIS. I think that is the effect which would be very unfortunate, but to my mind there is no such thing as an innocent purchaser of stocks — I mean innocent in the sense in which we are considering the purchasers of stock in the organization. It is entirely contrary, not only to our laws but what ought to be our whole attitude toward investments, that the person who has a chance of profit where, by going into an enterprise, or the chance of getting a larger return than he could get on a perfectly safe mortgage or bond, that he should have the chance of gain without any responsibility. The idea of such persons being innocent in the sense of not letting them take the consequences of their acts is, to my mind, highly immoral, and is bound to work out, if pursued, in very evil results to the community. When a person buys stock in the American Tobacco Co. and buys stock in the Standard Oil Co., and buys stock in any of those organizations of doubtful validity and of doubtful practices, they are not innocent; they are guilty constructively by law, and they should be deemed so by the community and held up to a responsibility; precisely to the same responsibility that the English owners of Irish estates should have been held up, although it was their bailiffs who were guilty of nearly every oppression that attended the absentee landlordism of Ireland. . . .

George E. Mowry: THEODORE ROOSEVELT AND THE PROGRESSIVE MOVEMENT

WHATEVER the sentiments of the Democrats, there was no doubt of the attitude of the thousand and some gathered in Chicago on August 5, 1912, to attend the first national Progressive convention. Stamped on their faces was an earnestness that often suggested fanaticism. From every part of America they came, with the reverential air of the consecrated. Strikingly absent were the crowds of "plug-uglies," ward bosses, and other avaricious specimens of the lower depths of politics which customarily swarm around a national convention.

From Theodore Roosevelt and the Progressive Movement by George E. Mowry. The University of Wisconsin Press, 1946. Reprinted by permission.

In their place was a group of well-dressed, serious citizens with the respectability of Sunday school superintendents. In fact, this was less a political convention than an assemblage of crusaders. To such a group had Peter the Hermit preached, and to such an audience had Garrison's *Liberator* thundered some seventy years before.

The tone of the body was in keeping with the character of its membership. There was little of the blaring brass bands or the noisy claques that punctuate the usual convention. The solemn gravity "was striking and impressive." All through the convention the delegates listened to the speakers with rapt faces. With each emotion-laden hour dedicated to social justice the delegates became more intense. Here and there both men and women were seen wiping tears from their eyes. And as the body reached the peaks of emotionalism it broke forth in the swelling strains of a hymn.

The moose has left the wooded hill; his call
  rings through the land.
It's a summons to the young and strong to join
  with willing hand:
To fight for right and country; to strike down
  a robber band,
And we'll go marching on.[1]

This was, indeed, progressivism militant. But when the convention roll was called some significant absences were noted. Missing were the dead Dolliver and Senator Cummins, who had made the creed of progressivism dominant in Iowa. Absent too were William E. Borah and George Norris, who had led the progressive fight in Congress for years. But most conspicuous was the absence

in this gathering of the liberal clans of Robert Marion La Follette, one of the very fathers of progressivism.

As if to balance these missing faces there were new leaders at Chicago — new and also strange leaders, at least for a reform gathering. Standing out among the other delegates were the two, George W. Perkins and Frank Munsey, whose money and support had made the Progressive party possible. Certainly their progressivism was at best of questionable character, and if there is any truth to the old saw that he who feeds a political party directs its policies, then the Progressive party faced an inevitable internal conflict. Side by side with the ardent devotees of reform at Chicago stood also the old-line bosses Flinn, Walter Brown, and Dan Hanna, who had already given evidence of their disbelief in the permanence of a reforming party. So little faith did Charles J. Bonapart have in Flinn's political integrity that he had advised against making him a member of the National Municipal League.[2] But even with such incongruities, the great gathering at Chicago was a monumental tribute to the spirit of reform and social consciousness that had been sweeping the country for a decade. It was also a testament of the faith of millions in the leadership of Theodore Roosevelt. . . .

A far more serious quarrel, which eventually drew in most of the leaders of the party, was one over the platform; in the end it went far to encompass the destruction of the organization. The dispute originated in part over the notorious disappearance of the anti-trust plank from the platform during the course of the convention. But the quarrel had a far more fundamental basis. Essentially it was a struggle for control between two

[1] *Chicago Tribune, New York Times,* and *New York World,* August 5, 6, 1912; *New York Sun, Philadelphia North American,* and *Kansas City Star,* August 6, 1912.

[2] Bonaparte to Clinton R. Woodruff, November 22, 1912, Bonaparte MSS.

groups in the party with conflicting ideologies. In another sense it was a struggle between nineteenth- and twentieth-century liberalism.

At one pole in this battle for factional supremacy stood George W. Perkins, financier of the party, a man whose expressed economic and social views coincided very closely with those of Roosevelt. For years prior to 1912 Perkins had attacked the theory behind anti-trust legislation. Intimately connected with the House of Morgan, Perkins advocated government regulation instead of government destruction. By 1912 he was advocating a federal regulatory body, similar in scope to the Interstate Commerce Commission, with the power to set prices on industrial goods. He closely concurred — vocally at least — in Roosevelt's desire to extend the regulative power of the federal government to protect the more submerged portions of the country's population from the ravages of industrial capitalism. Thus Perkins and Roosevelt stood together as exponents of a new paternalism which took sharp issue with historic individualism.

Many Progressives, however, still believed that a restoration of competition was possible and desirable. Most of these men came from west of the Appalachians. When they learned before the convention that Roosevelt opposed the inclusion of an anti-trust plank in the platform, they sent hot letters of protest to Oyster Bay. "Many Progressives contend for a restoration of competition, believing that it would be better for the country and more conducive to industrial progress," argued Senator Bristow.[3] Cummins, Clapp, Borah, and many others agreed with him. Not a few important leaders of the party doubly distrusted the

scheme for the regulation of business, especially when it came from the lips of Perkins. They doubted Perkins' progressivism and his fair intent. They disliked his power in the party. They feared that his gospel of regulation was the scheme of financial titans to get a strangle hold on the government. Voicing these apprehensions, Bristow asked Roosevelt, "In this scheme of regulation is there not a grave danger that 'big business' will more likely control the government than the government controlling big business?"[4]

This questioning of Perkins' regulatory doctrines and of their ultimate purpose crystallized into frank suspicion during the convention. Before the convention met Roosevelt had stated that he would continue to oppose the anti-trust proposal. In the Committee on Resolutions, however, a plank endorsing and strengthening the Sherman Law was passed after a sharp struggle. In part the statement read: "We favor strengthening the Sherman law by prohibiting agreements to divide territory or limit output; refusing to sell to customers who buy from business rivals; to sell below cost in certain areas while maintaining high prices in other places; using the power of transportation to aid or injure special business concerns; and other unfair trade practices."[5]

After the resolution had been adopted it was carried upstairs, where Roosevelt, Perkins, and Beveridge were engaged in supervising the work of the committee below. At once a debate started over Perkins' objections to the anti-trust section. Roosevelt later wrote that he had concurred with Perkins, but that they

---

[3] Joseph L. Bristow to Roosevelt, July 15, 1912, Roosevelt MSS.

[4] Bristow to Roosevelt, July 15, 1912, Roosevelt MSS.

[5] Claude G. Bowers, *Beveridge and the Progressive Era* (Boston, 1932), 431–432.

had both objected not to the endorsement of the anti-trust law but rather to the listing of prohibited practices on the ground that they would weaken the law. This defensive statement, however, did not coincide with either Roosevelt's previous or his subsequent statements on the Sherman Act. At any rate, the whole plank endorsing the act and not merely the enumeration of the specific practices was stricken out and sent back to the committee below. Just what happened in the lower room when the committee considered the revision is uncertain. Most of those present later remembered that the committee disapproved of striking out the clause and re-adopted it as it had been written originally. Roosevelt himself admitted later that such action had probably been taken inadvertently, although at the time he was told by Senator Dixon that the committee had approved the revised platform.[6]

The next day William Draper Lewis, in presenting the platform to the convention, included both the endorsement of the Sherman Law and the list of undesirable practices. As he did so, Perkins excitedly got to his feet. "That does not belong in the platform. We cut it out last night," he shouted to Amos Pinchot as he hurriedly left the hall. A conference of the party leaders was called at once. Roosevelt instructed O. K. Davis, secretary of the party, to delete the paragraph dealing with the Sherman Law. Accordingly, the platform was printed by the newspapers and later for campaign distribution without mentioning the Sherman Anti-Trust Law.[7] And thus the Pro-

gressive party opened itself to the campaign charge of attempting to legalize monopoly.

The omission of the Sherman plank was immediately denounced by many members of the party. Irately they charged that Perkins was responsible for the surreptitious guillotining. They had strongly protested against Perkins' connection with the party from the very beginning, and now their objections crystallized into rebellion. When the Progressive National Committee met, these men, led by William Allen White, the two Pinchots, and Meyer Lissner, tried to prevent the selection of Perkins as its chairman. But the financial godfather of the party, supported by Roosevelt, was too strong for them: after hours of debate he was duly elected. Later the committee even increased his power by authorizing Roosevelt and him to select the rest of the National Executive Committee. Momentarily after this setback the opposition to Perkins waned. But when the story of the anti-trust episode was noised around, all the misgivings returned. For the sake of unity during the campaign the opposition to Perkins remained silent. But silence emphatically did not give consent.[8] On the rest of the platform there was little disagreement. Long ago the leaders of the party had indicated their desires to Roosevelt. And since there was little hope of attracting any measure of conservative support, Roosevelt accepted most of the suggestions. He did not, however, consent to Gifford Pinchot's proposals for an imme-

[6] Roosevelt to Amos Pinchot, December 5, 1912, and to George L. Record, December 13, 1912, Henry F. Cochems to Roosevelt, November 16, 1912, Roosevelt MSS.

[7] Roosevelt to Amos Pinchot, December 5, 1912, and to George L. Record, December 13, 1912,

Roosevelt MSS.; Bowers, *Beveridge*, 440; O. K. Davis, *Released for Publication* (New York, 1925), 329–334.

[8] *Official Minutes of the Progressive National Committee*, 2; Meyer Lissner to George W. Perkins, August 5, 1912 (copy), Roosevelt MSS.; Bowers, *Beveridge*, 440; O. K. Davis, *Released for Publication*, 337–339.

diate national workingmen's compensa-
tion act and the creation of a department
of social welfare, or to a curious plan to
prevent the exportation of raw materials.
Neither would he accept a suggestion by
William Rockhill Nelson for the sociali-
zation of lawyers.[9] In the end, with a
few exceptions, the platform closely followed the lines Roosevelt had laid down
in his Confession of Faith. Altogether it
was perhaps the most radical platform
any major party had yet presented to the
electorate. Eugene V. Debs remarked
succinctly that the Progressives' ban-
danas had replaced the red flag of
socialism.[10]

Now the convention had only to nomi-
nate the president and vice-president before adjourning. And since Roosevelt
had selected Governor Johnson of Cali-
fornia as a running mate, the nomina-
tions were reduced to mere formalities.
At seven o'clock on Wednesday, August
7, Senator Beveridge, competing with
the wild cheers of the delegates, announced that Theodore Roosevelt and
Hiram Johnson had been nominated.
Shortly thereafter, Roosevelt and Johnson appeared before the convention.
Introduced by Beveridge, Roosevelt received a demonstration such as few men
have ever evoked. As he stepped forward to speak after the riotous acclaim
had died, the convention to a man broke
out into the fervent "Battle Hymn of the
Republic." Only in song could that sincere group of men and women indicate
just how much and how far they trusted
their leader.

Roosevelt was visibly shaken. In the
deep silence that followed his voice
trembled and for once he could find no

words. "I come forward," he said simply,
"to thank you from the bottom of my
heart for the great honor you have con-
ferred on me and to say that of course I
accept."

A few minutes later the convention
adjourned on a typical note. After the
notification speeches were over, the
whole body of delegates burst into song.
And as the last chords of the Doxology
faded away, Chairman Beveridge let his
gavel fall. The first national convention
of the Progressive party was at an end.[11]

The campaign that followed was a
stormy one. Almost before the convention had got under way the first salvo of
sharp criticism had been fired. Before it
ended the floodgates of denunciation
were wide open. The members of the
new party were described as "liars,"
"thieves," and "besmirchers of honest
men." Roosevelt was depicted as a "political anti Christ" whose swollen and
prurient ambition had led him beyond
the moral law, and whose promises were
as false as a dicer's oaths. The platform
of the new party, according to the conservative press, was not an orderly program of reform but a long wild call to
revolt. The Confession of Faith, screamed
the *New York Sun*, "is a manifesto of
revolution. It is a program of wild and
dangerous changes. It proposes popular
nullification of the Constitution. It proposes state socialism."[12]

President Taft, at least, added little to
the heat of the campaign. In accordance
with his announcement early in July that
under no conditions would he campaign
actively, he confined his efforts to a moderate acceptance speech and two or three
dignified public letters. In these few
efforts Taft reconciled his political posi-

[9] J. Franklin Fort to Roosevelt, July 29, 1912,
Roosevelt to William Rockhill Nelson, July 30,
1912, Roosevelt MSS.

[10] *New York Times*, August 14, 1912.

[11] *Chicago Tribune*, August 8, 1912.

[12] *New York Sun, New York Times,* and *New
York Herald*, August 7, 1912.

tion with his own true philosophical bent. For deep underneath he had always been a conservative. For a while in the first decade of the century, under the spell of the restless Roosevelt, he had thought of himself as a progressive and had even accepted the succession with the sincere intention of making advances on Roosevelt's liberal beginnings. But faced with the reality of office and with a widening fissure between conservative and progressive in his party, he had gradually found his true political level. Once there, he saw, perhaps to his surprise, clustered around him the Aldriches of the Republican party and not the Dollivers or the La Follettes.

Taft's campaign utterances of 1912 might well have come from the lips of Aldrich. In his acceptance speech on August 1 he deplored the reign of "sensational journalism" and the unrest of the people. He feared that social justice as then interpreted simply meant a "false division of property" which would approximate socialism. He denounced the recall of judges, the limitation of the power to grant injunctions, and trial by jury in contempt cases as vicious examples of class legislation designed to protect the lawless.[13] His later written views approached toryism. For in defending the high protective tariff, in calling for measures to restore business confidence, and in his allusions to the law of supply and demand as it worked its inevitable way on the labor market, the president was simply repeating the fifty-year-old shibboleths of organized reaction.[14]

In contrast to Taft, Roosevelt soon swung into a strenuous campaign of electioneering. Although he fully expected to lose the election and faced reluctantly

the arduous labors of the campaign, he stuck at it with all his old vigor.[15] A fortnight after his initial August campaign in New England he was in the Middle West. Two weeks later he was on the Pacific Coast, and by September 24 he was again in the Corn Belt. After a ten-day swing into the South he once again invaded the Northwest. While speaking in Milwaukee on October 14 he was shot by an insane man. From then until the last of October he rested, recovering from his wound.

As in the past Roosevelt's journeys through the country had been triumphal as a Roman warrior's. This was not the Roosevelt of 1900, for the years had left their mark. He was a bit slower in movement now, heavy around the waist; gray touched his temples. But he had lost none of his old power to attract the multitude. If anything, his manifest sincerity in 1912 and his ostensible abandonment of opportunism engendered even more devotion. At the opening of the campaign ten thousand people jammed the railroad station at Providence, Rhode Island, to welcome him. That night at Infantry Hall, with seats selling for a dollar apiece, thousands of people had to be turned away.[16] When he visited Los Angeles the entire city turned out. Business closed down, traffic was completely stopped, and two hundred thousand people lined the streets to cheer him as he rode from the station.[17]

Nor did the election lack the dramatic and the spectacular with which Roosevelt always managed to surround himself. The country grinned when it heard that "Teddy" had climbed over a tender

13 *New York Times,* August 2, 1912.

14 *Ibid.,* October 7, 1912.

15 Roosevelt to Arthur Lee, August 14, 1912, Roosevelt MSS.

16 *New York Times,* August 16, 1912.

17 *Kansas City Star,* September 16, 1912.

into the engine of a transcontinental express to run the train for a space and jar the passengers off their seats.[18] Even his enemies admired the mettle he displayed at Milwaukee when he insisted on continuing his speech after being dangerously wounded. Everyone applauded his magnanimity in protecting the would-be assassin from the fury of the bystanders. "Stand back. Don't hurt the man," he had shouted as the crowd rushed to avenge the deed.[19] Even with a bullet in his breast he could savor the drama, and his mind shrewdly dictated the best histrionic tactics. He clutched a bloody handkerchief, held up for all to see. A month later Roosevelt wrote to Earl Grey with revealing candor: "I would not have objected to the man's being killed at the very instant, but I did not deem it wise or proper that he should be killed before my eyes if I was going to recover."[20]

Throughout the campaign Roosevelt scarcely mentioned the president but centered most of his remarks on Woodrow Wilson. Setting aside his old weapons of irony and sharp sarcasm, he attacked his Democratic opponent with a gentle but devastating ridicule. Against the polished and literary phrases of his adversary, Roosevelt at least held his own. It was difficult for him to answer Wilson's charge that his election would mean the rule of the United States Steel Corporation through the mediation of Perkins.[21] Troublesome also was the prediction that the election of a Progressive president would cause legislative chaos, since the Congress would be Democratic or Republican. The renewed inquiry into cor-porate campaign contributions of 1904 may possibly have lost Roosevelt considerable support. Wilson scored heavily also when he attacked Roosevelt's faith in high protection. But in the polemics over two divergent philosophies of government Roosevelt was calling the tune of the times.

Espousing the tenets of Jeffersonian liberalism, Wilson had leveled one attack after another at the Rooseveltian concept of a master state almost without limit in its power to direct the economic life of the nation. He maintained that freedom of industrial activity was necessary for a healthy economic life. Roosevelt's program of regulation would inevitably lead to governmental sanctification of exploiting monopolies. What was needed was not the regulation of industrial combines but their dissolution under the Sherman Law and the restoration of a competitive basis. Such a bureaucratic state as Roosevelt envisaged would put an end to human liberty. "The history of liberty," remarked Wilson with his usual felicity, "is the history of the limitation of governmental power."[22]

Roosevelt, designating such doctrines as "rural toryism" and their author as a sincere doctrinaire who delighted in professorial rhetoric, replied that such a description was true of governments up until the advent of democracy, but not thereafter. For what have the people to fear, he asked, from a strong government which is in turn controlled by the people? If Wilson's doctrine meant anything, it meant "that every law for the promotion of social and industrial justice which has been put upon the statute books ought to be repealed."[23]

[18] New York Times, September 9, 1912.

[19] Ibid., October 15, 1912.

[20] November 15, 1912, Roosevelt MSS.

[21] New York World, October 9, 1912.

[22] New York Times, September 16, 1912.

[23] New York Sun, September 16, 1912.

But Roosevelt's most effective answer to his critics was in his last speech before sixteen thousand people jammed into Madison Square Garden. Leaving a sickbed to deliver it, he made in this redefinition of his principles his greatest speech of the campaign and one of the finest of his whole political career. As he stood on the platform men noticed that this was a new Roosevelt. For once he immediately tried to stop the cheering, which lasted, despite his efforts, for forty-five minutes. He used none of the old sarcasm or the belligerent personal attacks, and the pronoun *we* took the place of the overworked *I.*

"We are for human rights and we intend to work for them," he said in answer to the charges that the New Nationalism would lead straight to autocracy. "Where they can be best obtained by the application of the doctrine of states' rights, then we are for states' rights. Where in order to obtain them, it is necessary to invoke the power of the Nation, then we shall invoke to its uttermost limits that mighty power. We are for liberty. But we are for the liberty of the oppressed, and not for the liberty of the oppressor to oppress the weak and to bind the burdens on the shoulders of the heavy laden. It is idle to ask us not to exercise the powers of government when only by that power of the government can we curb the greed that sits in the high places, when only by the exercise of the government can we exalt the lowly and give heart to the humble and downtrodden."

And then in the last moments of the campaign Roosevelt took occasion to fire one more explosive shot at his old enemy the courts. "We stand for the Constitution, but we will not consent to make of the Constitution a fetich for the protection of fossilized wrong," he exclaimed.

"We recognize in neither court, nor Congress, nor President, any divine right to override the will of the people."[24]

As election day neared it was obvious that the real race would be between Roosevelt and Wilson. Taft could expect little support from the reforming members of the Republican party. Moreover, the president had alienated a large block of conservative supporters. Many industrial leaders who had voted the Republican ticket for years agreed with James M. Swank, president of the American Iron and Steel Association, that the president's tariff and trusts views were heretical.[25] For once a Republican administration was having a difficult time in collecting enough money to finance an election. When asked to contribute, H. C. Frick answered that he would give almost any amount to insure the success of the Republican party but that he did not care to contribute to this campaign because the administration "utterly failed to treat many of its warmest friends fairly."[26]

As Taft's defeat became more patent with the days, so-called sober conservatism, fearing a Roosevelt victory, dipped its pen in hysterical and malicious abuse. Branding Roosevelt as the American Mahdi and his followers as wild dervishes, the *New York Sun* predicted that once Roosevelt gained the White House he would never depart. "As the Emperor Sigismund was above grammar, so is Theodore Rex above recall, except that

24 *New York Times,* October 31, 1912.

25 James M. Swank to Joseph B. Foraker, May 15, 1912, Foraker to J. G. Schurman, November 19, 1912, Foraker MSS., Library of Congress; *Washington Post,* August 18, 1912.

26 Henry C. Frick to Charles D. Hilles, November 2, 1912, in George Harvey, *Henry Clay Frick* (New York, 1928), 310.

of his promises and his principles."[27] The *New York World* joined in the chorus by predicting that a second term would lead to a third, and a third straight to a tyrant.[28] *Harper's Weekly* had long before warned the country that Roosevelt's election would be followed within ten years by a bloody revolution and the subsequent rule of a despot.[29]. But the depths of scurrility and foolishness were plumbed by George Harvey in an editorial entitled "Roosevelt or the Republic." "Roosevelt was the first President," it began, "whose chief personal characteristic was mendacity, the first to glory in duplicity, the first braggart, the first bully, the first betrayer of a friend who ever occupied the White House." From there it went on with equally bitter adjectives, referring to Roosevelt's "perpetual lying," his "shameless treatment of helpless women," and his willingness to grind the American people under the iron boot. "It is not the foreign war," the editorial concluded, "so commonly anticipated as a consequence of Roosevelt's accession to the dizzy height of unrestrained authority that makes for dread; it is the civil strife that would almost inevitably ensue from patriotic resistance to usurpation by a half mad genius at the head of the proletariat."[30]

Those unreasoning charges might well have remained unwritten; for a Roosevelt victory was next to impossible. Since Wilson's nomination precluded any great migration of progressives from the Democratic party, Roosevelt had to depend upon the support of Republican progressives. They were not enough. Beyond that, traditional progressivism in the Republican party, unlike the make-up of the Democratic party, had always flourished in the agrarian sections of the country. There Roosevelt was handicapped by the fact that many of the progressive Republican leaders in the western sections of the country were either opposed to him or were content in giving him meager support from outside the ranks of the Progressive party.

Roosevelt's paternalistic philosophy of government was not agrarian but urban in its appeal. A high protective tariff, the regulation of industrial monopolies, the long list of labor reforms, offered little to the farmer. In fact the New Nationalism, in almost every instance, was the antithesis of the physiocratic, low-tariff, trust-busting doctrine of the farming West. It is little wonder then that in the eighteen largest cities of the country Roosevelt polled a considerably greater proportion of the total vote than he did throughout the agricultural regions.[31] He was supported in the West not because of his New Nationalism but in spite of it.

27 *New York Sun*, September 25, 1912.

28 *New York World*, November 2, 1912.

29 *Harper's Weekly*, June 1, 1912.

30 *North American Review*, 195: 433–438 (October 12, 1912).

31 In the eighteen largest cities of the country Roosevelt obtained thirty-five per cent of the total vote, Wilson forty-one, and Taft twenty-three, whereas in the country at large Roosevelt received twenty-five per cent, Wilson forty-five, and Taft twenty-five.

Walter Lippmann: DRIFT AND MASTERY

IN the last thirty years or so American business has been passing through a reorganization so radical that we are just beginning to grasp its meaning. At any rate for those of us who are young today the business world of our grandfathers is a piece of history that we can reconstruct only with the greatest difficulty. We know that the huge corporation, the integrated industry, production for a world market, the network of combinations, pools and agreements have played havoc with the older political economy. The scope of human endeavor is enormously larger, and with it has come, as Graham Wallas says, a general change of social scale.[1] Human thought has had to enlarge its scale in order to meet the situation. That is why it is not very illuminating to say, for example, that the principles of righteousness are eternal and that the solution of every problem is in the Golden Rule. The Golden Rule in a village, and the Golden Rule for a nation of a hundred million people are two very different things. I might possibly treat my neighbor as myself, but in this vast modern world the greatest problem that confronts me is to find my neighbor and treat him at all. The size and

[1] See The Great Society, by Graham Wallas, for a psychological analysis of this change of social scale. I had the privilege of reading Mr. Wallas's book in manuscript while I was revising this one. My obligations go far deeper than that, however, for they extend back to the spring of 1910, when Mr. Wallas came from England to lecture at Harvard. In A Preface to Politics I tried to express my sense of the way in which Graham Wallas marks a turning point in the history of political thinking.

From *Drift and Mastery* by Walter Lippmann. Henry Holt and Company, 1914. Reprinted by permission.

intricacy which we have to deal with have done more than anything else, I imagine, to wreck the simple generalizations of our ancestors. After all, they were not prophets, and the conservative to-day makes an inhuman demand when he expects them to have laid out a business policy for a world they never even imagined. If anyone thinks that the Fathers might have done this let him sit down and write a political economy for the year 1950.

"Since the Sherman Act was passed (1890)," says President Van Hise of Wisconsin University, "a child born has attained its majority." Indeed he has, much to the surprise of the unwilling parents. Now a new business world has produced a new kind of business man. For it requires a different order of ability to conduct the Steel Trust, than it did to manage a primitive blast-furnace by means of a partnership. The giant corporation calls for an equipment unlike any that business has ever known: the minds of the managers are occupied with problems beyond the circle of ideas that interested the old-fashioned chop-whiskered merchants. They have to preserve intimate contact with physicists and chemists, there is probably a research laboratory attached to the plant. They have to deal with huge masses of workingmen becoming every day more articulate. They have to think about the kind of training our public schools give. They have to consider very concretely the psychology of races, they come into contact with the structure of credit, and a money squeeze due to the Balkan war makes a difference in their rate of output. They have to keep thousands of ignorant stockholders somewhere in the back of their mind, people who don't know the difference between puddling and pudding. They may find themselves an issue in a political campaign, and if they are to be successful they must estimate correctly the social temper of the community. Diplomacy is closely related to the selling department, and perhaps at times they may have to dabble in Latin-American revolutions.

Mr. Louis D. Brandeis commented on this change of scale in his testimony before the Committee on Interstate Commerce.[2]

Anyone who critically analyzes a business learns this: that success or failure of an enterprise depends usually upon one man. . . . Now while organization has made it possible for the individual man to accomplish infinitely more than he could before, aided as he is by new methods of communication, by the stenographer, the telephone, and system, still there is a limit for what one man can do well . . . When, therefore, you increase your business to a very great extent, and the multitude of problems increases with its growth, you will find, in the first place, that the man at the head has a diminishing knowledge of the facts, and, in the second place, a diminishing opportunity of exercising careful judgment upon them.

In this statement, you will find, I believe, one of the essential reasons why a man of Mr. Brandeis's imaginative power has turned against the modern trust. He does not believe that men can deal efficiently with the scale upon which the modern business world is organized. He has said quite frankly, that economic size is in itself a danger to democracy. This

means, I take it, that American voters are not intelligent enough or powerful enough to dominate great industrial organizations. So Mr. Brandeis, in company with many important thinkers the world over, has turned de-centralizer. The experience of history justifies his position in many respects: there is no doubt that an organization like the Holy Roman Empire was too large for the political capacity of human beings. It is probably true that the Morgan empire had become unwieldy. It may be that the Steel Trust is too large for efficiency. The splendid civilizations of the past have appeared in small cities. To-day if you go about the world you find that the small countries like Belgium, Holland, Denmark, are the ones that have come nearest to a high level of social prosperity. I once heard George Russell (Æ), the Irish poet and reformer, say that an ideal state would be about the size of County Cork.

Yet it is not very helpful to insist that size is a danger, unless you can specify what size.

The senators asked Mr. Brandeis that question. They pressed him to state approximately what percentage of an industry he considered an effective unit. He hesitated between ten per cent and forty per cent, and could not commit himself. Obviously, — for how could Mr. Brandeis be expected to know? Adam Smith thought the corporations of his day doomed to failure on the very same grounds that Mr. Brandeis urges against the modern corporation. Now the million dollar organization is not too large for efficiency and the billion dollar one may be. The ideal unit may fall somewhere between? Where? That is a problem which experiments alone can decide, experiments conducted by experts in the new science of administration.

The development of that science is the only answer to the point Mr. Brandeis raises. Remarkable results have already been produced. Every one of us, for example, must wonder at times how the President of the United States ever does all the things the papers say he does. When, for example, does the man sleep? And is he omniscient? The fact is that administration is becoming an applied science, capable of devising executive methods for dealing with tremendous units. No doubt the President with his increasing responsibilities is an overworked man. No doubt there are trusts badly administered. No doubt there are inflated monopolies created for purely financial reasons. But just what the limits of administrative science are, a legislature is no more capable of determining than was Mr. Brandeis. Only experience, only trial and ingenuity, can demonstrate, and in a research so young and so swift in its progress, any effort to assign by law an arbitrary limit is surely the most obvious meddling. Say to-day that one unit of business is impossible, to-morrow you may be confronted with an undreamt success. Here if anywhere is a place where negative prophecy is futile. It is well to remember the classic case of that great scientist Simon Newcomb, who said that man would never fly. Two years before that statement was made, the Wright brothers had made secret flights.

It may well be that the best unit is smaller than some of the modern trusts. It does not follow that we must break up industry into units of administration whose ideal efficiency is spent in competing with one another. I can understand, for example, the desire of many people to see Europe composed of a larger number of small nations. But I take it that everyone wishes these small nations to coöperate in the creation of a common European civilization. So it is with business. The unit of administration may be whatever efficiency demands. It may be that the steel industry would gain if it were conducted by forty corporations. But at the same time there are advantages in common action which we cannot afford to abandon. Technical improvement must be for the whole industry, the labor market must be organized and made stable, output must be adjusted to a common plan. The appearance of federal organization seems to suggest a possible compromise in which the administrative need for decentralization is combined with the social demand for a unified industrial policy.

No one, surely, proposes to revive the little business monarch who brooded watchfully over every operation in factory and office, called his workingmen by their pet names, and was impelled at almost every turn by Adam Smith's "natural propensity to truck and barter." For just as in political government "the President" does a hundred things every day he may never even hear of, just as the English Crown acts constantly through some unknown civil servant at $1,500 a year, — so in big business, — the real government is passing into a hierarchy of managers and deputies, who, by what would look like a miracle to Adam Smith, are able to coöperate pretty well toward a common end. They are doing that, remember, in the first generation of administrative science. They come to it unprepared, from a nation that is suspicious and grudging. They have no tradition to work with, the old commercial morality of the exploiter and profiteer still surrounds these new rulers of industry. Perhaps they are unaware that they are revolutionizing the discipline, the incentives, and the vision of the business world. They do brutal and stupid things, and their essential work is obscured. But they are conducting business on a scale without precedent in history.

The real news about business, it seems to me, is that it is being administered by men who are not profiteers. The managers are on salary, divorced from ownership and from bargaining. They represent the revolution in business incentives at its very heart. For they conduct gigantic enterprises and they stand outside the higgling of the market, outside the shrewdness and strategy of competition. The motive of profit is not their personal motive. That is an astounding change. The administration of the great industries is passing into the hands of men who cannot halt before each transaction and ask themselves: what is my duty as the Economic Man looking for immediate gain? They have to live on their salaries, and hope for promotion, but their day's work is not measured in profit. There are thousands of these men, each with responsibilities vaster than the patriarchs of industry they have supplanted. It is for the commercial theorists to prove that the "ability" is inferior, and talent less available.

It is no accident that the universities have begun to create graduate schools of business-administration. Fifty years ago industry was an adventure or perhaps a family tradition. But to-day it is becoming a profession with university standing equal to that of law, medicine, or engineering. The universities are supplying a demand. It is big business, I believe, which has created that demand. For it is no longer possible to deal with the present scale of industry if your only equipment is what men used to call "experience," that is, a haphazard absorption of knowledge through the pores.

Just as it is no longer possible to become a physician by living with doctors, just as law cannot be grasped by starting as a clerk in some attorney's office, so business requires a greater preparation than a man can get by being a bright, observant, studious, ambitious office boy, who saves his money and is good to his mother.

What it will mean to have business administered by men with a professional training is a rather difficult speculation. That is a very far-reaching psychological change, I have no doubt. The professions bring with them a fellowship in interest, a standard of ethics, an esprit de corps, and a decided discipline. They break up that sense of sullen privacy which made the old-fashioned business man so impervious to new facts and so shockingly ignorant of the larger demands of civilized life. I know that the professions develop their pedantry, but who was ever more finicky, more rigid in his thinking than the self-satisfied merchant? It would be idle to suppose that we are going suddenly to develop a nation of reasonable men. But at least we are going to have an increasing number of "practical" men who have come in contact with the scientific method. That is an enormous gain over the older manufacturers and merchants. They were shrewd, hard-working, no doubt, but they were fundamentally uneducated. They had no discipline for making wisdom out of their experience. They had almost no imaginative training to soften their primitive ambitions. But doctors and engineers and professional men, generally, have something more than a desire to accumulate and outshine their neighbors. They have found an interest in the actual work they are doing. The work itself is in a measure its own reward. The instincts of workmanship, of control over brute things, the desire for order, the satisfaction of services rendered and uses created, the civilizing passions are given a chance to temper the primal desire to have and to hold and to conquer.

* * *

It has been said that no trust could have been created without breaking the law. Neither could astronomy in the time of Galileo. If you build up foolish laws and insist that invention is a crime, well — then it is a crime. That is undeniably true, but not very interesting. Of course, you can't possibly treat the trusts as crimes. First of all, nobody knows what the trust laws mean. The spectacle of an enlightened people trying in vain for twenty-five years to find out the intention of a statute that it has enacted — that is one of those episodes that only madmen can appreciate. You see, it is possible to sympathize with the difficulties of a scholar trying to decipher the hieroglyphics of some ancient people, but when statesmen can't read the things they've written themselves, it begins to look as if some imp had been playing pranks. The men who rule this country to-day were all alive, and presumably sane, when the Sherman Act was passed. They all say in public that it is a great piece of legislation — an "exquisite instrument" someone called it the other day. The highest paid legal intelligence has concentrated on the Act. The Supreme Court has interpreted it many times, ending with the enormous assumption that reason had something to do with the law. The Supreme Court was denounced for this: the reformers said that if there was any reason in the law, the devil himself had got hold of it. As I write, Congress is engaged in trying to define what it thinks it means by the Act. . . .

That uncertainty hasn't prevented a mass of indictments, injunctions, lawsuits. It has, if anything, invited them. But of course, you can't enforce the criminal law against every "unfair" business practice. Just try to imagine the standing army of inspectors, detectives, prosecutors, and judges, the city of courthouses and jails, the enormous costs, and the unremitting zeal — if you cannot see the folly, at least see the impossibility of the method. To work with it seriously would not only bring business to a standstill, it would drain the energy of America more thoroughly than the bitterest foreign war. Visualize life in America, if you can, when the government at Washington and forty-eight state governments really undertook not our present desultory pecking, but a systematic enforcement of the criminal law. The newspapers would enjoy it for a week, and everybody would be excited; in two weeks it would be a bore; in six, there would be such a revolt that everyone, radical and conservative, would be ready to wreck the government and hang the attorney-general. For these "criminal" practices are so deep in the texture of our lives; they affect so many, their results are so intimate that anything like a "surgical" cutting at evil would come close to killing the patient.

If the anti-trust people really grasped the full meaning of what they said, and if they really had the power or the courage to do what they propose, they would be engaged in one of the most destructive agitations that America has known. They would be breaking up the beginning of a collective organization, thwarting the possibility of coöperation, and insisting upon submitting industry to the wasteful, the planless scramble of little profiteers. They would make impossible any deliberate and constructive use of our natural resources, they would thwart any effort to form the great industries into coordinated services, they would preserve commercialism as the undisputed master of our lives, they would lay a premium on the strategy of industrial war, — they would, if they could. For these anti-trust people have never seen the possibilities of organized industries. They have seen only the obvious evils, the birth-pains, the undisciplined strut of youth, the bad manners, the greed, and the trickery. The trusts have been ruthless, of course. No one tried to guide them; they have broken the law in a thousand ways, largely because the law was such that they had to.

At any rate, I should not like to answer before a just tribunal for the harm done this country in the last twenty-five years by the stupid hostility of anti-trust laws. How much they have perverted the constructive genius of this country it is impossible to estimate. They have blocked any policy of welcome and use, they have concentrated a nation's thinking on inessentials, they have driven creative business men to underhand methods, and put a high money value on intrigue and legal cunning, demagoguery and waste. The trusts have survived it all, but in mutilated form, the battered makeshifts of a trampled promise. They have learned every art of evasion — the only art reformers allowed them to learn.

It is said that the economy of trusts is unreal. Yet no one has ever tried the economies of the trust in any open, deliberate fashion. The amount of energy that has had to go into repelling stupid attack, the adjustments that had to be made underground — it is a wonder the trusts achieved what they did to bring

order out of chaos, and forge an instrument for a nation's business. You have no more right to judge the trusts by what they are than to judge the labor movement by what it is. Both of them are in that preliminary state where they are fighting for existence, and any real outburst of constructive effort has been impossible for them.

But revolutions are not stopped by blind resistance. They are only perverted. And as an exhibition of blind resistance to a great promise, the trust campaign of the American democracy is surely unequalled. Think of contriving correctives for a revolution, such as ordering business men to compete with each other. It is as if we said: "Let not thy right hand know what thy left hand doeth; let thy right hand fight thy left hand, and in the name of God let neither win." Bernard Shaw remarked several years ago that "after all, America is not submitting to the Trusts without a struggle. The first steps have already been taken by the village constable. He is no doubt preparing a new question for immigrants" . . . after asking them whether they are anarchists or polygamists, he is to add " 'Do you approve of Trusts?' but pending this supreme measure of national defense he has declared in several states that trusts will certainly be put in the stocks and whipped."

There has been no American policy on the trust question: there has been merely a widespread resentment. The small local competitors who were wiped out became little centers of bad feeling: these nationally organized industries were looked upon as foreign invaders. They were arrogant, as the English in Ireland or the Germans in Alsace, and much of the feeling for local democracy attached itself to the revolt against these national despotisms. The trusts made enemies right and left: they squeezed the profits of the farmer, they made life difficult for the shopkeeper, they abolished jobbers and travelling salesmen, they closed down factories, they exercised an enormous control over credit through their size and through their eastern connections. Labor was no match for them, state legislatures were impotent before them. They came into the life of the simple American community as a tremendous revolutionary force, upsetting custom, changing men's status, demanding a readjustment for which people were unready. Of course, there was anti-trust feeling; of course, there was a blind desire to smash them. Men had been ruined and they were too angry to think, too hard pressed to care much about the larger life which the trusts suggested.

This feeling came to a head in Bryan's famous "cross of gold" speech in 1896. "When you come before us and tell us that we shall disturb your business interests, we reply that you have disturbed our business interests by your action. . . . The man who is employed for wages is as much a business man as his employers. The attorney in a country town is as much a business man as the corporation counsel in a great metropolis. The merchant at the crossroads store is as much a business man as the merchant of New York. The farmer . . . is as much a business man as the man who goes upon the Board of Trade and bets upon the price of grain. The miners . . . It is for these that we speak . . . we are fighting in the defense of our homes, our families, and posterity." What Bryan was really defending was the old and simple life of America, a life that was doomed by the great organization that had come into the world. He thought he was fighting the plutocracy: as a matter of fact he was fighting something much deeper than

that; he was fighting the larger scale of human life. The Eastern money power controlled the new industrial system, and Bryan fought it. But what he and his people hated from the bottom of their souls were the economic conditions which had upset the old life of the prairies, made new demands upon democracy, introduced specialization and science, had destroyed village loyalties, frustrated private ambitions, and created the impersonal relationships of the modern world.

Bryan has never been able to adjust himself to the new world in which he lives. That is why he is so irresistibly funny to sophisticated newspaper men. His virtues, his habits, his ideas, are the simple, direct, shrewd qualities of early America. He is the true Don Quixote of our politics, for he moves in a world that has ceased to exist.

He is a more genuine conservative than some propertied bigot. Bryan stands for the popular tradition of America, whereas most of his enemies stand merely for the power that is destroying that tradition. Bryan is what America was; his critics are generally defenders of what America has become. And neither seems to have any vision of what America is to be.

Yet there has always been great power behind Bryan, the power of those who in one way or another were hurt by the greater organization that America was developing. The Populists were part of that power. La Follette and the insurgent Republicans expressed it. It was easily a political majority of the American people. The Republican Party disintegrated under the pressure of the revolt. The Bull Moose gathered much of its strength from it. The Socialists have got some of it. But in 1912 it swept the Democratic Party, and by a combination of circumstances, carried the country.

The plutocracy was beaten in politics, and the power that Bryan spoke for in 1896, the forces that had made muckraking popular, captured the government. They were led by a man who was no part of the power that he represented.

Woodrow Wilson is an outsider capable of skilled interpretation. He is an historian, and that has helped him to know the older tradition of America. He is a student of theory, and like most theorists of his generation he is deeply attached to the doctrines that swayed the world when America was founded.

But Woodrow Wilson at least knows that there is a new world. "There is one great basic fact which underlies all the questions that are discussed on the political platform at the present moment. That singular fact is that nothing is done in this country as it was done twenty years ago. We are in the presence of a new organization of society. . . . We have changed our economic conditions, absolutely, from top to bottom; and, with our economic society, the organization of our life." You could not make a more sweeping statement of the case. The President is perfectly aware of what has happened, and he says at the very outset that "our laws still deal with us on the basis of the old system . . . the old positive formulas do not fit the present problems."

You wait eagerly for some new formula. The new formula is this: "I believe the time has come when the governments of this country, both state and national, have to set the stage, and set it very minutely and carefully, for the doing of justice to men in every relationship of life." Now that is a new formula, because it means a willingness to use the power of government much more extensively.

But for what purpose is this power to be used? There, of course, is the rub. It is to be used to "*restore* our politics to their full spiritual vigor *again*, and our national life, whether in trade, in industry, or in what concerns us only as families and individuals, to its purity, its self-respect, and its *pristine* strength and freedom." The ideal is the old ideal, the ideal of Bryan, the method is the new one of government interference.

That, I believe, is the inner contradiction of Woodrow Wilson. He knows that there is a new world demanding new methods, but he dreams of an older world. He is torn between the two. It is a very deep conflict in him between what he knows and what he feels.

His feeling is, as he says, for "the man on the make." "For my part, I want the pigmy to have a chance to come out". . . "Just let some of the youngsters I know have a chance and they'll give these gentlemen points. Lend them a little money. They can't get any now. See to it that when they have got a local market they can't be squeezed out of it." Nowhere in his speeches will you find any sense that it may be possible to organize the fundamental industries on some deliberate plan for national service. He is thinking always about somebody's chance to build up a profitable business; he likes the idea that somebody can beat somebody else, and the small business man takes on the virtues of David in a battle with Goliath.

"Have you found trusts that thought as much of their men as they did of their machinery?" he asks, forgetting that few people have ever found competitive textile mills or clothing factories that did. There isn't an evil of commercialism that Wilson isn't ready to lay at the door of the trusts. He becomes quite reckless in his denunciation of the New Devil —

Monopoly — and of course, by contrast the competitive business takes on a halo of light. It is amazing how clearly he sees the evils that trusts do, how blind he is to the evils that his supporters do. You would think that the trusts were the first oppressors of labor; you would think they were the first business organization that failed to achieve the highest possible efficiency. The pretty record of competition throughout the Nineteenth Century is forgotten. Suddenly all that is a glorious past which we have lost. You would think that competitive commercialism was really a generous, chivalrous, high-minded stage of human culture.

"We design that the limitations on private enterprise shall be removed, so that the next generation of youngsters, as they come along, will not have to become protégés of benevolent trusts, but will be free to go about making their own lives what they will; so that we shall taste again the full cup, not of charity, but of liberty, — the only wine that ever refreshed and renewed the spirit of a people." That cup of liberty — we may well ask him to go back to Manchester, to Paterson to-day, to the garment trades of New York, and taste it for himself.

The New Freedom means the effort of small business men and farmers to use the government against the larger collective organization of industry. Wilson's power comes from them; his feeling is with them; his thinking is for them. Never a word of understanding for the new type of administrator, the specialist, the professionally trained business man; practically no mention of the consumer — even the tariff is for the business man; no understanding of the new demands of labor, its solidarity, its aspiration for some control over the management of business; no hint that it may be necessary to organize the fundamental industries of the country on some definite plan so that our resources may be developed by scientific method instead of by men "on the make"; no friendliness for the larger, collective life upon which the world is entering, only a constant return to the commercial chances of young men trying to set up in business. That is the push and force of this New Freedom, a freedom for the little profiteer, but no freedom for the nation from the narrowness, the poor incentives, the limited vision of small competitors, — no freedom from clamorous advertisement, from wasteful selling, from duplication of plants, from unnecessary enterprise, from the chaos, the welter, the strategy of industrial war.

Alpheus Thomas Mason: LOUIS D. BRANDEIS:
Spotlighting the Trusts, 1911-1912

BRANDEIS could accept neither the Old Guard Republicanism of Taft, nor the pseudo-Progressivism of Roosevelt. He felt keenly the need for a united Progressive party, of members drawn from the ranks of both older parties, so as to reflect the real issues. The chance that such a party would emerge to carry through the measures for which he had long been agitating appeared now to have been thwarted by the loyalties of practical politics and the fascination of political rhetoric. If only there could be a clear-cut division between reaction and progress instead of "the issue of T.R.!"

That clear-cut division did not exist in the Republican party; if it existed in the nation at all, it was only between Republicans and Democrats — especially after the Democrats at their convention in Baltimore on July 2, 1912, nominated Woodrow Wilson, the Governor of New Jersey, for President. The next day Brandeis wrote La Follette: "I know that you will be delighted with the action of Bryan and the Baltimore Convention, as you think so well of both Bryan and Wilson. It seems to me that those Progressives who do not consider themselves bound by party affiliations ought to give Wilson thorough support, not only to insure his election, but to give him all the aid and comfort which he will need to maintain the Progressive position which he has assumed and to carry out the Progressive policies. I wish I might have a chance to talk this over with you soon."

Here was a new chance. The Progressives had lost the Republican nomination; they could still win the election with a Democrat.

Brandeis had never met or even seen the Democratic candidate, but from all he had heard of Wilson, he seemed to have the qualities of a Progressive leader. The Democratic party, moreover, had taken a strong stand for Progressive principles. In a resolution introduced by William Jennings Bryan the party had renounced any affiliation with "the privilege-hunting and favor-seeking class," and with any Democrats in that class. The resolution practically read out of the party by name such financiers as Thomas Fortune Ryan and August Belmont. For Brandeis, this confirmed the party's determination to "drive the money lenders out of the temple." His fervent hope of 1910 seemed now to be fulfilled: "If only there were a Democratic party. What havoc would be wrought!"

Brandeis urged all good Progressives to rally to Wilson's banner. That seemed to him the only course for Progressives — for La Follette men, Roosevelt men, Democrats, and even some Taft men. If Progressives fought Wilson, there was the chance of a two-term reactionary Taft administration, a noisy but futile Roosevelt administration, or a Wilson administration made impotent by lack of support. But if Progressives rallied behind Wilson and conservative Democrats went over to Taft, party lines would be drawn realistically and Brandeis's hope of a clear issue between Conservatism and Progressivism would be realized. Accordingly, Brandeis publicly came out for Wilson:

His nomination ranks among the most encouraging events in American history . . . for he possesses in a high degree the qualities of an effective progressive leader. . . . He understands the dangers incident to the control of a few of our industries and finance. He sees that true democracy and social justice are unattainable unless the power of the few be curbed, and our democracy become industrial as well as political. . . . But the struggle of privilege for privilege is unending and omnipresent. That struggle is as subtle as it is determined. The struggle will not close when Wilson is elected. We may be sure that every effort he may make as President to carry out the Progressive policies will meet the stubborn resistance from the possessors and apostles of privilege. . . . The progressive cause can succeed only if it has loyal support from the progressives. It can fail only if the progressives fail in their duty of giving Wilson their full support.

In taking his stand with Wilson, Brandeis parted company with many old friends and colleagues. Both Gifford Pinchot and George Rublee expressed their regret at his decision. Rublee wrote him on July 18: "I grieve that you are not to be in the new (Roosevelt) party, because I think it needs you more than perhaps any other man."

"T.R. is pretty near irresistible," Brandeis commented on reading that his friend Henry Moskowitz had joined the Progressive party. But Brandeis stood firm, believing that T.R. was leading "not the Progressive party but a Roosevelt party."

Brandeis's shifts in political allegiance from Taft to La Follette, and then to Wilson, were later used to discredit him.

Actually he was entirely consistent in the terms of his one dominating purpose — to put through essential reforms. He was not interested in political sectarianism and evangelism. He wanted things done progressively and objectively. He had no concern with partisanship. Parties, groups, and individual political figures were to him but tools for putting constructive ideas into effect. In the shifting currents of politics, men and political organizations had to be used and discarded as conditions of the moment demanded. His frequent statements that he was not a political man were in a sense true. When he took part in campaign fights and put his influence behind one candidate or another, it was only as a means to an end, and the personalities involved were only incidentally important. This attitude was, of course, modified sometimes by personal loyalties, as in the case of his faithful adherence to La Follette. The campaign of 1912, however, was for him chiefly a search for the best vehicles by which to put his economic proposals into effect.

The Campaign Begins

Brandeis's direct relation with Wilson began on August 1, 1912, when he wrote the candidate: "This morning's news that you will suggest dealing with the tariff by reducing the duties gradually at the rate of 5 per cent a year is further evidence that the country may expect from you a wisely progressive administration. The simple plan which you suggest is true statesmanship; and the real tariff reformers should rally to your support."

To this letter Wilson replied: "Your letter of August first has given me a great deal of pleasure. I have been very much cheered and reassured by the knowledge of your approval and support. I sincerely hope that the months to come will draw us together and give me the benefit of many conferences with you."

Late in August, Brandeis received a telegram from Charles R. Crane, saying that Wilson would like to see him. Accordingly, on August 27, he took a night boat to New York, ate breakfast at the Albermarle Hotel, visited the Democratic Headquarters in New York, and rode down to Sea Girt, New Jersey. There, on the afternoon of the 28th, the People's Attorney and the Democratic presidential nominee had lunch and a three-hour talk. They discussed social and industrial problems, chiefly the trust question, which promised to be the leading issue of the campaign. Apparently each man was impressed with the other. After the meeting Brandeis wrote of Wilson: "It seems to me that he has the qualities for an ideal President — strong, simple, and truthful, able, open-minded, eager to learn and deliberate."

A major part of the Sea Girt conference was given to exploring the weaknesses of Roosevelt's party (Brandeis and Wilson conceded Taft the conservatives) and planning how to exploit those weaknesses in the campaign. This was not hard to do. The principles of Roosevelt's party as enunciated at Chicago were the antithesis of those Brandeis had been advocating. Under Roosevelt, industrial problems were to be resolved by having business "be good"; the "inevitable" trend toward monopoly was not to be interfered with; attacks on business under the Sherman Anti-Trust Act would cease; wicked practices in business would be restrained or punished; labor would be aided by "welfare" measures. In short, the Bull Moose platform was the gospel of gentility in politics. Dominant in its administration would be corporation executives like Perkins and Munsey, who were Roosevelt's chief lieutenants, aided by such assorted gentlemen and ladies as

Harold L. Ickes, Boss Bill Flinn, Professor Charles E. Merriam, and Jane Addams. They had great hopes, but first they would have to get in.

Roosevelt's spokesmen tried to becloud the campaign by defining the issues between T.R. and Wilson as regulation versus destructive, wasteful competition. Brandeis, however, dissipated the confusion with a question which summed up the real difference between the two parties: "Shall we regulate competition or monopoly?" His work was creating some trouble for the enemy, and there was more trouble ahead.

Soon after his August vacation began, Normal Hapgood invited him to define the campaign issues for *Collier's*. He finally consented, though Hapgood found it "hard work" persuading him to give up any part of his vacation. "*Entre nous,* I have Norman supplied with editorials through the October 19 number," he wrote Alfred, September 15, "and shall probably add two more to make the full measure." In these editorials as well as in articles published under his own name, he directed public attention to flaws in the Roosevelt-Perkins scheme for "domesticating" the modern industrial monsters. In proposing not only to legalize monopoly as the future policy, but also to condone past violations of law, the New Party, he maintained, was advocating a course which must seriously undermine respect for law. Already the failure of proceedings against the Oil and Tobacco Trusts gave substance to his belief that the law did not operate with equal effect on rich and poor, and if "flagrant violations of law and ethics" as practiced by the trusts were thus to be given legal sanction, it would shake the legal foundations of the community. Aside from pointing out the economic and social disadvantages of monopoly, which he had so long expounded, Brandeis called attention to certain practical difficulties in the New Party's program. He knew from experience the limits of regulation. Any pious hope that trusts could be harnessed to the general welfare by helpfully regulatory commissions was certain to be disappointed. The I.C.C., which dealt mainly with one type of industry, and that practically uniform throughout the country, was overworked and ineffective. What supermen would be required to understand the details of thousands of totally different businesses in America! He pointed out, moreover, that the I.C.C. had been unable to control power monopolies, notably the New Haven. Its greatest success had been as regulator of competition.

While lambasting the New Party's program, Brandeis also struck at its sponsors. His major target was Perkins, whose Progressive professions contrasted awkwardly with his business affiliations. In fact, Perkins's presence as chairman of the executive committee and financial mainstay of the Roosevelt party perhaps aroused more suspicion than anything else. His dominant influence in the party embarrassed and disillusioned intelligent Progressives such as Amos Pinchot, who wrote Brandeis, October 8, in the middle of the campaign: "I regret more than I can tell you that George Perkins and Frank Munsey are taking so prominent a place in our party. Munsey is painting us, as he has no right to do, as the party of protection, while Perkins is giving people an opportunity to assume that we are the defenders of the trusts. This makes me pretty sick, for I feel that the great majority of the people who have gone in with us are right-thinking and unselfish."

Privately Brandeis described Perkins as a "menace to the country." In an editorial prepared for *Collier's* he released such a barrage against him that Mark

Sullivan objected to it strongly and Hapgood had to soften it. "Isn't the Progressive party trying to serve both God and Mammon?" Brandeis was fond of saying. "Think of Jane Addams on the one hand and George Perkins on the other — 'two props of virtue for a Christian prince to stay him from the fall of vanity.'"

While most of the fire was concentrated on the "prime minister" of the New Party, Brandeis did not spare its monarch. He resented T.R.'s decision to run and believed that in taking that course Roosevelt himself became the major obstacle to Progressive triumph. He was convinced that but for the overweening vanity of the Rough Rider, Republican Progressives would have joined Democratic Progressives and captured the Democratic party. As time went on, his feeling became more and more intense. "The more I think of T.R.'s performances, the angrier I get," he had written Alfred on August 31. "It will be an interesting test of the American people to see whether he gains on them this trip." He was inclined to agree with the *New York World* that there were "two overwhelming reasons" for the election of Wilson — Roosevelt and Taft. Gleefully he adopted Clark Howell's paraphrase of Teddy's famous peroration: "We meet at Armageddon to battle for the trusts."

Brandeis's contrasts of Roosevelt and Wilson were particularly effective. The Progressive movement had been fortunate, he agreed, in having T.R. as its leader when it was in the stage of "agitation." The Rough Rider possessed exactly the qualities then needed — "the qualities of the great preacher — emotion, imagination, the dramatic sense and dash . . . not only to arouse men but to create a following." In 1912, however, these qualities were outmoded. A large majority of the American people were aware of existing abuses and the Progressives had become powerful enough to compel the adoption of remedies. Not the warrior, but the constructive statesman was now needed: "We need, in addition to the manly virtues and a quick intelligence, that student quality of diligent, patient inquiry; that true open-mindedness which makes one willing to listen, as well as to speak; and that calm, careful, hard thinking which is essential to sound judgment on legislation. . . . We need the will to labor, as well as the power to achieve." The press, he contended, was under a peculiar obligation in this campaign, to draw the clear distinction between "a man of substance" and "a man of noise."

Though aware that the success of Progressive reform in coming years depended much on the personality of the Chief Executive, Brandeis's attention, as usual, was centered on measures and policies. Wilson relied heavily on him for a definition of the Democratic party's stand on major economic issues, wiring him on September 28: "Please set forth as explicitly as possible the actual measures by which competition can be effectively regulated. The more explicit we are on this point the more completely will the enemies' guns be spiked." In his reply of September 30 Brandeis outlined the "fundamental and irreconcilable" difference between the economic policy of Democrats and of Bull Moosers. The two parties were agreed as to a government commission to regulate business, but the policies which such a commission would administer under the two parties were at opposite poles. The issue between them, as he defined it, was the "difference between industrial liberty and industrial absolutism, tempered by government (that is, party) supervision."

The Democrats would maintain competition where it existed and restore it where it had been crushed. They believed that "no methods of regulation ever have been or can be devised to remove the menace in private monopoly and overweening commercial power." The New Party, on the other hand, "does not fear commercial power, however great, if only methods for regulation are provided." Furthermore, it insisted that private monopoly might in many cases be desirable, or in any case, was inevitable, and that trusts should not be dismembered, but should be made "good" by regulation.

Specifically, the Democratic program, while applauding the Sherman Act as embodying a declaration of sound economic policy, called for utilizing twenty-two years' experience under the act to improve the effectiveness of its enforcement. A bill drawn up by Brandeis had been, as we have seen, introduced in Congress by Senator La Follette and Representative A. O. Stanley, and this pointed the line of action. The necessary steps consisted in removing the uncertainties of the Sherman Act by defining practices which unreasonably restrained trade, facilitating its enforcement by the courts, and creating a commission to aid in administering the law. Brandeis's detailed memorandum went on to tell Wilson how these things could be accomplished.

Stumping for Wilson

Brandeis did not confine himself to writing, counseling, and serving as "idea man." The Democratic National Committee arranged a speaking tour for him, covering New England, New York, Ohio, Illinois, Michigan, and Pennsylvania, and in mid-September he once again took the stump. He spoke mostly before economic clubs and Chambers of Commerce, on his favorite subject — the trusts. He attacked the New Party's platform, and elaborated specific measures of reform. Of T.R.'s platform he was accustomed to observe: "The superstructure is beautiful; but the foundations are fatally defective."

Before the state A.F. of L. at Fitchburg, Massachusetts, September 18, 1912, he thoroughly dissected T.R.'s labor plank. He expressed great admiration for its broad scope and clear language, but observed that the very care with which it had been constructed emphasized its glaring weakness. It pledged the party to social justice and to fourteen measures for improving the condition of the working man. These Brandeis himself heartily approved. But it omitted the one thing without which all else was worthless. Nowhere could he find a hint of the party's unqualified endorsement of labor's *right to organize*. This omission, he pointed out, was the more significant, because the party accepted and defended the trusts, whose labor policy had but one objective — "extermination of organized labor." The mere promise that the trusts would be regulated was no guarantee that their labor policy would be liberalized. Brandeis concluded: "Legislation and commissions — like God — help only 'him who helps himself'; and a social program which accepts these things as a substitute for industrial liberty, instead of using them as a means of securing industrial liberty, is fundamentally unsound. You know perfectly well that no legislation, even when sustained by the court — and no commission, though able and honest — will effectually protect labor, unless the workingmen and public opinion are behind them."

Brandeis's analysis was challenged on September 23 by the *Boston Journal*, which charged him with "misrepresentation of the facts." The paper asserted that he "could not have read the platform," and insisted that he correct his statement. He must have made a mistake, the *Journal* maintained, because the New Party's platform said plainly enough: "We favor the organization of the workers, men and women, as a means of protecting their interests and of promoting their progress." Brandeis in a letter to the editor on September 26 replied that nowhere in that carefully phrased plank was the *right* to organize mentioned. He explained that a right means "something that the law protects," and he showed how a recent decision of the United States Supreme Court (Adair v. U.S., 208 U.S. 161) upheld the right of corporations to discharge workers for joining a union. How, therefore, could the trusts complacently "favor the organization of the workers" and at the same time rely on the prevailing law, and on their own strength, to prevent it? What the New Party's attitude amounted to, he said, was: "I am in favor of the law but against its enforcement."

Brandeis concluded his rebuke to the editor of the *Journal* with a pithy expression of his own attitude on labor: "The New Party with its program of a few specific and desirable measures which would mitigate some of the evils of existing industrial conditions, is purposing only to take a certain paternal care of the American workingman, who, if given a fair field, could, in the main, take care of himself."

The argument most frequently used to defend monopoly was the so-called wastefulness of competition. But, said Brandeis, the wastefulness of competition is like the wastefulness of democracy. In a speech at Providence he elaborated this theme:

The wastes of democracy are among the greatest obvious wastes, but we have compensations in democracy which far outweigh that waste, and make it more efficient than absolutism. So it is with competition. Incentive and development which are incident to the freer system of business result in so much greater achievement that the waste is relatively insignificant. The margin between that which men naturally do, and that which they can do, is so great that a system which urges men on to action and develops individual enterprise and initiative is preferable, in spite of the wastes that necessarily attend that process.

Besides, Brandeis pointed out, Wilson proposed to eliminate many of the wastes of competition by regulating it. This would not mean fostering artificial conditions in industry; on the contrary, it was the suppression of competition by the great trusts that had created artificial conditions. To regulate competition meant to remove those spurious competitive practices which destroyed it — the methods of the prize ring, he called them. "Competition should be regulated so that it may be protected," and he compared his position to that of the man "who loved peace so much that he was willing to fight for it."

Brandeis's campaign speeches were so hard-hitting that he was urged for his own political interest to soften his blows. Some Progressives were considering him for the Senate, and he was therefore cautioned that "the leaders of the present Progressive party may be led to believe that the difference between your trust policy and that of most Progressives . . . is more vital than in fact is . . . the case." To this Brandeis replied:

I have been disposed to think that the path of duty for me does not lead to any public office, and I as yet see no reason for changing that opinion. On the other hand, I feel that the duty is very clear that I should utilize that insight which participation in practical affairs has given me to prevent well-meaning Progressives from being led into the belief that private monopoly is desirable or permissible, provided it be regulated.

That issue seems to me to be a fundamental one — one on which the New Party is radically wrong, and so long as it stands for private monopoly and privilege, it cannot be the true means of real progress in this country.

Perhaps Brandeis's most effective campaign speech was before the Cleveland Chamber of Commerce on October 15. The day before, Roosevelt had been shot and slightly wounded by a fanatic in Milwaukee, and Brandeis promptly turned the incident to advantage. The attempted assassination was a symptom, he observed, of the declining respect for law in the United States. And what were the reasons for the decline? One was the fact that the law, as administered, did not express the will of the American people. He went on:

See what the effect would be upon the American people, to find . . . that in the year 1912, a political party and a large number of people standing for the best interests of America come forward and declare, "Let us legalize the trust, let us legalize that which under existing law has grown up illegally, because it is impossible, or possibly undesirable, to prevent private monopoly."

If that position, gentlemen, became the accepted policy of America, we would declare, in substance, that not only vested rights but vested wrongs were to be supreme in this country. And there could be nothing to my mind which would so threaten the welfare of America and imperil everything that we are working for, that we prize today, as the solemn declaration of the inability of this government to carry out the will which the people have registered in an act of Congress. . . .

. . . We have been trifling with the people. . . . Jeeringly, jokingly, year after year, we have smiled over the inefficiency of that expression of the people's will, which there (in the Sherman Act) and elsewhere has gone upon the statute books to satisfy a popular demand.

It is, gentlemen, that sort of thing which is bringing on the Los Angeles and Lawrence and Milwaukee incidents, and which, if not corrected and corrected in the right manner, will endanger all our institutions. To secure respect for law, we must make the law respectable.

Brandeis was proud of the speech, thought it was a great success. He wrote Alfred about it: "I gave them a real sermon on respect for law apropos the T.R. incident, working it around to the trusts and I think I rather held them.". . .

Suggestions for Additional Reading

For those who would like to know more about Theodore Roosevelt's life and career, Henry Pringle's *Theodore Roosevelt* (New York, 1931), is unquestionably the best biography available both in respect to readability and critical judgment. Roosevelt's *Autobiography* (New York, 1913) is valuable for his own estimate of his activities as well as a compendium of his ideas on a variety of subjects. For most students, however, the most usable collection of Rooseveltian ideas is the *Theodore Roosevelt Cyclopedia*, edited by Albert Bushnell Hart and Herbert Ronald Ferleger (New York, 1941). This volume is a careful encyclopedic arrangement of ideas expressed by Theodore Roosevelt in correspondence and speeches in topics ranging from "Abbey Theatre" to "Young Men's Christian Association."

The best short biography of Woodrow Wilson is Herbert C. F. Bell's *Woodrow Wilson and the People* (Garden City, N. Y., 1945). Also useful for this problem is Ray Stannard Baker's *Woodrow Wilson, Life and Letters* (New York 1927–1939), particularly volumes I–III. Most useful is Arthur S. Link's penetrating study of Wilson's early political career and intellectual development, *Wilson, the Road to the White House* (Princeton, 1947). William Diamond's *The Economic Thought of Woodrow Wilson* (Baltimore, 1943), is an excellent study of a very important aspect of Wilson's thinking throughout his life and career which no careful student should overlook.

A good collection of Wilson's public writings is that of Ray Stannard Baker and William E. Dodd, *The Public Papers of Woodrow Wilson* (New York, 1925), particularly volumes I–V.

There are many autobiographical works which offer much interesting material on this fascinating period. Among these are such works as Robert M. La Follette, *La Follette's Autobiography* (Madison, 1913); Lincoln Steffens, *Autobiography* (New York, 1931); Frederick C. Howe, *The Confessions of a Reformer* (New York, 1925); Ray Stannard Baker, *American Chronicle* (New York, 1945); and Oswald Garrison Villard, *Fighting Years* (New York, 1939). Also helpful for an understanding of the period are such biographies as Henry Pringle, *The Life and Times of William Howard Taft* (2 vols., New York, 1939); Claude Bowers, *Beveridge and the Progressive Era* (New York, 1932); and Philip Jessup, *Elihu Root* (2 vols., New York, 1938).

Two outstanding special studies of the progressive period are Harold Underwood Faulkner's *The Quest for Social Justice, 1898–1914* (New York, 1931), which stresses social developments, and Matthew Josephson's, *The President Makers* (New York, 1940), which emphasizes political developments. Also, no present-day student should overlook the chapters on Roosevelt and Wilson in Richard Hofstadter's *The American Po-*

litical Tradition and the Men Who Made It (New York, 1948).

For those students who would like to go further with some of the seminal political thinking of the period Herbert David Croly's *The Promise of American Life* (New York, 1909), is indispensable. Also important in this regard are Charles R. Van Hise, *Concentration and Control* (New York, 1912); Walter E. Weyl, *The New Democracy* (New York, 1912); and Louis D. Brandeis, *Other People's Money* (New York, 1914).

Finally, no one should miss the opportunity to browse through such periodicals of the period 1910–1912 as: *Atlantic Monthly, Collier's,* the *Independent, Nation, Outlook, American Review of Reviews,* and *World's Work.* These contain many excellent articles on the trust problem as well as other problems of twentieth century democracy which will give the reader an interesting sample of the level of popular awareness of social and political questions at the time of the campaign of 1912.